You Are the Earth

YOU ARE THE EARTH

David Suzuki

and KATHY VANDERLINDEN

Art by WALLACE EDWARDS · Diagrams by Talent Pun

 David Suzuki Foundation

 GREYSTONE BOOKS
D&M PUBLISHERS INC.
Vancouver/Toronto/Berkeley

Greystone Books
An imprint of D&M Publishers Inc.
2323 Quebec Street, Suite 201
Vancouver, BC Canada V5T 4S7
www.greystonebooks.com

David Suzuki Foundation
2211 West 4th Avenue, Suite 219
Vancouver, BC Canada V6K 4S2

Library and Archives Canada Cataloguing in Publication
Suzuki, David, 1936–
You are the earth : know your world so you can make
it better / David Suzuki and Kathy Vanderlinden;
illustrator, Wallace Edwards.
Co-published by: David Suzuki Foundation.
Includes index.
Previous ed. published with title: You are the earth,
from dinosaur breath to pizza from dirt.
Reading grade level: 4–6. · Interest age level: 9–12.
ISBN 978-1-55365-476-6 (pbk.)

1. Human ecology—Juvenile literature.
2. Ecology—Juvenile literature. 3. Natural history—
Juvenile literature. I. Vanderlinden, Kathy II. Edwards,
Wallace III. David Suzuki Foundation IV. Title.

QH541.14.S92 2010   J577   C2009-907541-5

Mixed Sources
Cert no. SGS-COC-003548
© 1996 FSC
FSC

Editing by Nancy Flight
Cover and text design by Naomi MacDougall
Cover art by Wallace Edwards
Diagram art by Talent Pun
Printed and bound in China
by C&C Offset Printing Co., Ltd.
Text printed on acid-free, FSC-certified paper
Cover printed on FSC-certified paper
Distributed in the U.S. by Publishers Group West

We gratefully acknowledge the financial support of
the Canada Council for the Arts, the British Columbia
Arts Council, the Province of British Columbia
through the Book Publishing Tax Credit, and the
Government of Canada through the Canada Book
Fund for our publishing activities.

Credits

Myths and legends were based on the following
sources: "Out of the Sky" from Michael J. Caduto and
Joseph Bruchac, *Keepers of the Earth: Native Stories and
Environmental Activities for Children* (Saskatoon, SK:
Fifth House Publishers, 1991); "The Animal Canoe"
from "Tales of the Heroes" in Jan Knappert and Fran-
cesca Pelizzali, *Kings, Gods & Spirits from African
Mythology* (Vancouver/Toronto: Douglas & McIntyre,
1986); "The Gift of the Spider Woman" from B.C.
Sproul, *Primal Myths: Creating the World* (New York:
Harper & Row, 1979), and "Lifting Up the Sky" from
"Pushing Up the Sky" in Richard Erdoes and Alfonso
Ortiz, *American Indian Myths and Legends* (New York:
Pantheon Books, 1984).

Contents

Acknowledgments

The authors would like to thank the following people for their generous contributions to this edition: Aryne Sheppard and Laura Plant of the David Suzuki Foundation and Colin Carlson, Alison Lee, Katelyn Morran, Destiny Gulewich, Rachel Perrella, Neely Swanson, Kari Jo Kinley, Lorrie Anne Marsh, Ian Lai, Klara Marsh, Malykh Lopez, Patrisse Chan, and Patrick Ruvalcaba. Special thanks to our incomparable editor, Nancy Flight; to designer Naomi MacDougall and art director Peter Cocking; and to Wallace Edwards and Talent Pun for their stunning artwork.

In addition, the authors acknowledge the tremendous contribution of Amanda McConnell, who cowrote *The Sacred Balance,* on which this book is based. Thanks go also to the following for their help: David Barnum of West Sechelt Elementary School, Sechelt, B.C.; Gordon Li of Marlborough School, Burnaby, B.C.; Susan Martin of Delta Resource Centre, Delta, B.C.; Chuck Heath of Ridgeway Elementary School, North Vancouver, B.C.; Elliot M. Fratkin, Associate Professor of Anthropology, Smith College, Northampton, Mass.; Quentin Mackie, Assistant Professor of Anthropology, University of Victoria; Robert S. Schemenauer, Cloud Physicist, Environment Service, Environment Canada; Y.N. (Kenny) Kwok, Associate Professor of Physiology, University of British Columbia; and Peter Shin, Department of Nutritional Sciences, Faculty of Medicine, University of Toronto.

About This Book

The very first thing I remember happened when I was four years old. My dad and I were going on a camping trip, and he took me to a sporting goods store to buy a tent. He found a little pup tent he liked and set it up on the floor of the store. Then we both crawled in and lay down together to make sure there was enough room for both of us. The prospect of going camping was so exciting to me that I've never forgotten that moment. It was the beginning of my lifelong love of nature and of my dream that I would someday become a naturalist and travel to exotic places to collect animals.

When I grew up, I did become a scientist who studied nature. My work was filled with the wonder of discovery. But in the 1960s, I started hearing reports of dangers threatening the natural world. We humans were thoughtlessly polluting the air, destroying lakes and rivers, killing off entire groups of animals and their habitats, and putting our whole environment—our home—at risk. We weren't doing this on purpose; in trying to make a living, we just didn't think enough about these consequences. Like many people at that time, I began working with others to get laws passed to protect the environment.

In the late 1970s, I found myself in the Queen Charlotte Islands off the north coast of British Columbia. The Haida people who live on these islands call them Haida Gwaii. For thousands of years, the forests had provided shelter and food for the Haida people. But now the trees were also valuable as logs for the forestry industry. So for years a struggle had been going on between the forestry companies and the Haida.

While I was in Haida Gwaii, I met a Haida artist named Guujaaw. Since many loggers were Haida, and since forestry companies brought money into the Haida community, I asked him why he was against the logging. Guujaaw said, "If they cut all the trees down, of course we Haida will still be here. But then we'll be like everybody else."

His answer changed the way I looked at the world. I realized he was saying that the Haida people don't think of trees as just part of their landscape—they are part of the people, too. Those islands—along with the salmon, ravens, cedars, and ocean—make the Haida who they are. If the forests are cut down, a large part of what makes the Haida people special will be lost.

In the years since that conversation, I have met and worked with Aboriginal people around the world. And everywhere people say, "The Earth is our mother." As a scientist, I have come to understand that they are right. We are made of water, air, and the food we eat from the Earth's soil. I've realized that it is a mistake to think of the environment as something "out there," separate from us. We *are* the Earth.

The problem with so many battles about the environment is that we get caught up in debates that force us to choose between two valuable things—spotted owls *or* jobs, logging *or* parks, people *or* wildlife. When problems are put that way, someone or something will lose. But if we care about the coming generations, we can't have any losers. We have to decide what is really important and all work together for a better future.

I wrote this book to show what we need to survive—clean air, water, soil, the sun's energy, our wonderful variety of plant and animal life, love, and spirit. The challenge is to create societies and ways of life based on fulfilling those needs.

I hope that by reading this book you discover what you can do to meet those needs and learn some interesting things about yourself and the Earth. Open your eyes, mind, and heart to the beauty of the world. Then you can help make it a better place for yourself and all the other children who will inherit it.

David Suzuki
Vancouver, British Columbia

1 WALKING ON AIR

YOU PROBABLY DON'T think much about air. You can't see it, hear it, or grab a handful of it. It's almost as if it weren't there. And yet it's just about the most precious thing in the world.

Try holding your breath for five minutes. Can you do it? Of course not. Your body won't let you. You can try to hold your breath until your face turns red and purple, but the muscles in your lungs and chest will soon force you to breathe. That's how much your body needs air.

From the first breath you took when you were born to your last, you must have air. If you didn't have air for just five or six minutes, you would die. All of us Earthlings—people, animals, and plants—need air to live. And the amazing thing is, not only does air keep us alive, but it also ties us together. It's as if we are all swimming in an "air soup." When you breathe out, atoms—tiny, invisible particles—of air fly out of your nose and go right up the noses of all the people near you!

11

You're Breathing Dinosaur Breath

Did you know that the next breath you take will contain dinosaur breath? It sounds weird, but it's true. Here's how it works. Air is really a mixture of several gases. A gas is a light, invisible substance that floats freely in the air—water vapor or steam, for example. Two of these gases, nitrogen and oxygen, make up almost all of the air.

What's in the Air?

Air is mostly nitrogen and oxygen. Argon, carbon dioxide, and eight other gases together make up only about 1 percent of the air. The percentages here don't add up to exactly 100 percent because they are rounded off.

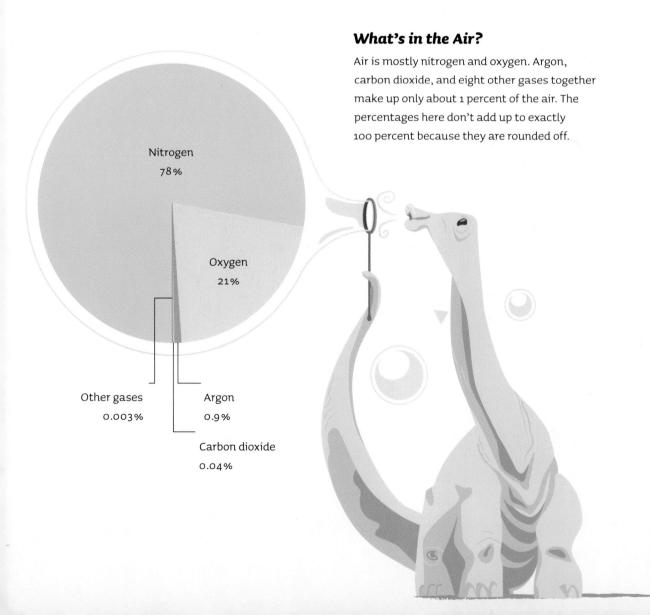

Nitrogen
78%

Oxygen
21%

Other gases
0.003%

Argon
0.9%

Carbon dioxide
0.04%

There is only a small amount of the gas argon in the air. Yet an American astronomer named Harlow Shapley calculated that each breath you breathe out, or exhale, contains about 30,000,000,000,000,000,000,000 (you can call that 30 zillion) atoms of argon.

In a few minutes, the atoms you've exhaled in that one breath will travel right through your neighborhood. In a year, they will have spread all around the Earth, and about 15 of them will be right back where they started—in your nose—every time you breathe.

Argon is always in you and around you. And not just in you but also in your best friend, your favorite pop star, the birds, snakes, flowers, trees, and worms. All of us air breathers are sharing in that same "pool" of argon atoms.

So here's where the dinosaurs come in. An interesting thing about argon atoms is that they never change or die—they stay around forever. That means that thousands of years ago, an Egyptian slave building the pyramids breathed some of the same argon atoms that later Joan of Arc, Napoleon, and Napoleon's horse breathed. And some of those were argon atoms exhaled by dinosaurs that lived 70 million years ago. They all breathed out argon atoms into the air—ready for you to breathe in as you read this sentence. And when you exhale your next 30 zillion argon atoms, some of them will one day find their way into the noses of babies not yet born.

What's true of argon is true of air in general. Air joins together all of Earth's creatures—past, present, and future.

Out of the Sky

The Onondaga people tell this legend.

L ONG BEFORE the Earth was formed, everything was water. Water
stretched in every direction, and in it swam all the fish, birds, and other
animals. High up above the water was Skyland, where a beautiful tree
with great white roots grew.

Skyland was ruled by an ancient chief who had a young wife. One night
she dreamed that the great tree had been uprooted. When she told her
strange dream to the chief, he was very sad.

"That is a powerful dream," he said. "When someone has such a powerful
dream, it is our way to try to make that dream come true."

And so the chief wrapped his arms around the trunk of the tree and began
to pull. He sweated and strained, and finally the roots gave way, leaving a
huge hole. The chief's wife leaned over the hole and looked down. There,

far below, she thought she saw something glistening. She grabbed one of the tree's branches for support and leaned over farther. Suddenly she lost her balance and fell through the hole. As she fell down, down, she held in her hand some seeds she had pulled from the tree.

Meanwhile, the animals below looked up.

"Somebody is falling out of Skyland," said a bird.

Right away, two swans flew up and caught the chief's wife in their great wings. As they brought her gently down to the water, they let her rest on their backs.

"She is not like us," said one of the swans. "I don't think she can swim or breathe under water. What should we do?"

"I know," said one of the water birds. "I have heard there is Earth far down beneath the water. If someone goes down and pulls up the Earth, then the Sky Lady will have a place to stand."

One after another, the animals and birds and fish dove as far down as they could go. But each time, they came up empty-handed.

Finally, a small voice said, "I will get the Earth or die trying."

It was Muskrat. She was not as big and powerful as some of the other animals, but she had a lot of courage. So Muskrat swam down, down, down. She swam so far down that she thought her lungs would burst. But still she swam deeper. Finally, just as her breath ran out, she reached down and touched something. When she floated up to the surface, she held a few bits of Earth in her paw.

"She has the Earth!" the animals shouted in excitement. "Now, where should we put it?"

"Put it on my back," said the Great Turtle. And so it was done. Immediately the bits of Earth grew bigger and bigger until they became the world. The swans set Sky Lady down on the Earth. As her feet touched the ground, she let the seeds fall out of her hand. Where they fell, trees, grass, and flowers sprang up. And so life began on Earth.

Take a *Deep* Breath...

Imagine Steve Nash pounding down the basketball court, dribbling the ball at top speed. It's a pretty impressive show, especially when you realize he is also filtering the air with his lungs. Each minute, he's taking 40 to 60 breaths and pumping 4 to 6 liters (quarts) of air through his lungs.

Your body has a wonderful system for getting air into every part of your body and making sure it's as pure as possible when it gets there. Even when you're not running and jumping like Steve but just hanging out, you take about 10 breaths a minute, or 600 an hour.

Think of what happens when you take one breath. Air enters your nose and gets filtered by tiny hairs lining the inside. They trap large dust particles and other bits that shouldn't get into your lungs. These bits will be expelled when you sneeze or blow your nose.

As the air rushes along the nasal chamber, getting warmed and moistened, it passes the olfactory bulb. This area sends messages to the brain about the odor of the air coming in. You're not as good at smelling as a dog is (a dog can tell one person from another by smell), but you're pretty good. You can tell if there are roses in the room, if dinner is burning on the stove, or if someone's wearing sweaty socks.

Next the air rushes down your windpipe and into the bronchi, or branches, of your lungs. Bronchi are tubes that split into smaller tubes called bronchioles, which keep branching out. At the very ends of the smallest bronchioles are air sacs, like tiny balloons. You have about 300 million of these air sacs in your lungs. If they were flattened out, they could cover the area of Steve Nash's basketball court!

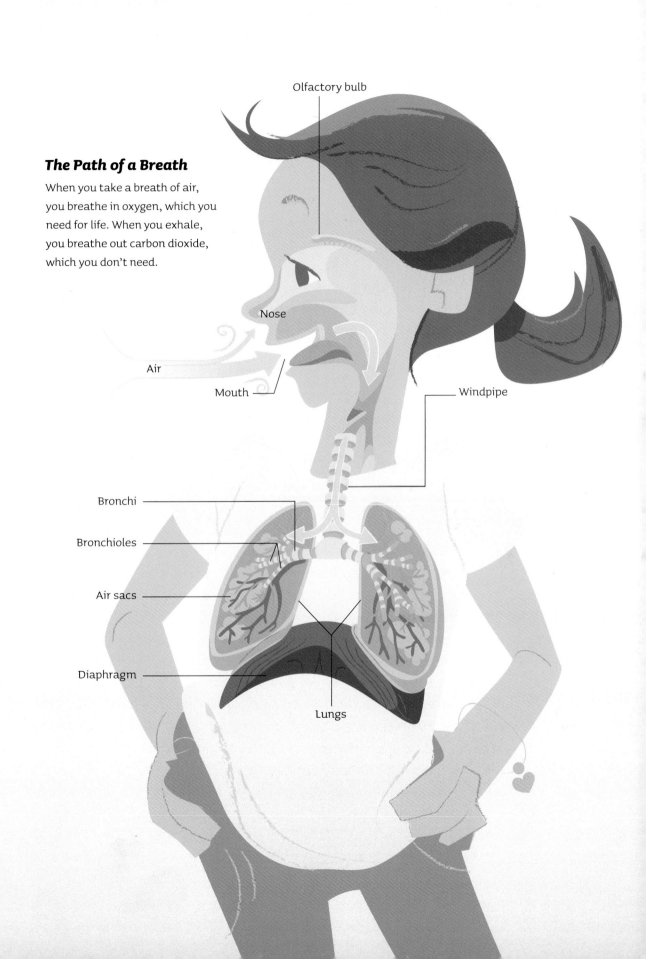

The Path of a Breath

When you take a breath of air, you breathe in oxygen, which you need for life. When you exhale, you breathe out carbon dioxide, which you don't need.

Olfactory bulb

Nose

Air

Mouth

Windpipe

Bronchi

Bronchioles

Air sacs

Diaphragm

Lungs

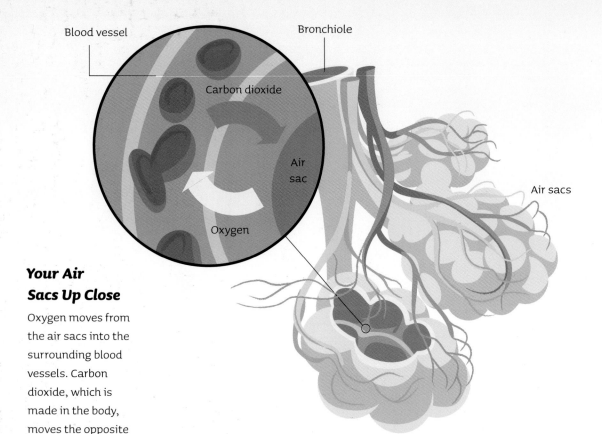

Blood vessel

Bronchiole

Carbon dioxide

Air sac

Air sacs

Oxygen

Your Air Sacs Up Close

Oxygen moves from the air sacs into the surrounding blood vessels. Carbon dioxide, which is made in the body, moves the opposite way—from the blood vessels into the air sacs. From there it is breathed out.

When the air gets to the sacs, it passes through their walls into your blood vessels. Air has now become part of your body, ready to go to work for you. The oxygen in the air is the most important gas—the one you must have to live. Every tissue and organ, especially your heart and brain, needs a constant supply of oxygen to do its job. So oxygen is carried in your bloodstream throughout your body.

While all of this is going on, the gas carbon dioxide is being formed as a waste product of body processes, such as digestion. Your body doesn't need carbon dioxide, so it gets rid of most of it. Carbon dioxide travels the same route as oxygen, only backwards—from your blood to your lungs to your nose, where you exhale it into the outside air. And it all happens automatically. You don't have to think about it because your body breathes for you, even when you are asleep.

Even when you breathe out, air remains in you and is always part of you. And the air you exhale becomes part of everyone nearby, too. Air connects us all.

How Air Got to Be Perfect

Earth's air has exactly the right mixture of gases you need to live. How do you think this perfect arrangement came to be? Let's imagine we could board a timeship and go back about 2.5 billion years, as life was just beginning to take hold on Earth.

Stepping out of the timeship, we look around. We see a landscape of rock and murky water, with no trees or plants or even soil anywhere. But we don't have time to explore, because in two minutes we're dead! Why? Because the air has almost no oxygen in it. Not only that, the temperature is so high we're roasted.

Or we would be, but fortunately we're wearing heat-protector suits and oxygen masks. We walk along and come to an ocean. Our suits are also equipped for deep-sea diving, and we've brought underwater microscopes to help us see super-tiny things. We dive down to the ocean floor and find a world of strange microscopic creatures. There are beings with tails that whip them along and others with rows of little bristles moving like oars. Some creatures have shells, and others have tiny harpoons to capture food.

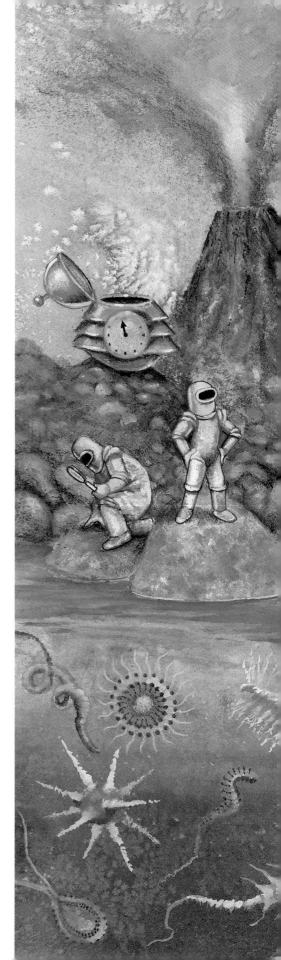

Extra-Fresh Air

Plants can help purify the air in a room by absorbing some of the chemical gases given off by paint, varnish, and glue.

Mixed into this zoo are some blue-green creatures, the ancestors of plants. They don't have leaves, seeds, or flowers yet, but like all plants they have learned how to make their own food. They do this by trapping the energy in sunlight. Then they combine that energy with water and carbon dioxide to produce a simple sugar—their food. This process is called photosynthesis. It also produces oxygen, which is necessary for life. Over many millions of years, these tiny, plantlike forms have slowly released oxygen into the water and air. But the air still contains too little oxygen to support any but the smallest, simplest creatures.

Back in the timeship, we travel forward several hundred million years. Now when we step outside, things are more interesting. The Earth's crust has been moving, draining oceans and exposing their plant-rich floors. Plants have been able to spread across the land. There are all kinds of plants, and they're all releasing oxygen into the air. Now we can take off our oxygen masks and just breathe. Because the temperature is cooler, we can also take off our heat-protector suits.

Magic Green Air Cleaners

Plants are essential to life on Earth. They take in carbon dioxide from the air and release oxygen through photosynthesis. In this way, plants provide oxygen for the world.

Plants take in carbon dioxide and release oxygen.

Carbon dioxide

Carbon dioxide

Water

Oxygen

Animals take in oxygen and release carbon dioxide.

Sugar

Sugar

Looking around, we see animals, too. First, microscopic animals and then larger ones have evolved to feed on the plants. The animals are breathing in oxygen and breathing out carbon dioxide. The plants are taking in carbon dioxide and releasing oxygen. What a great, harmonious system!

Let's get back in our timeship for one last trip forward to our own time. Now we can see a vast array of different plants and trees. They are still taking in carbon dioxide and supplying the air with oxygen. Billions of years ago they changed the Earth's air by sending oxygen into it. By doing so, they created the essential conditions for life in all its glorious forms.

Earth's Air Blanket

How high do you think the air goes? As high as the moon and stars? No way. Remember Steve and his basketball? Suppose that basketball were the Earth. If you wound a sheet of plastic wrap tightly around the ball, that sheet would represent the thickness of the air where we live and where weather happens.

That layer of air, called the troposphere, reaches only about 11 kilometers (7 miles) above the Earth—that's about the height at which planes fly. Beyond that is the rest of the Earth's atmosphere, the mixture of gases that surrounds the planet. The entire atmosphere stretches 2400 kilometers (1500 miles) into space, but the amount of gas decreases the farther out you go. Plants and animals can only live in the troposphere—the part of the atmosphere we usually mean when we say "air." It has exactly the right mixture of gases, exactly the right temperature, and exactly the right air pressure that living things need. This thin sheet of life-giving air is all we have to keep us breathing. So we should never take this precious air for granted.

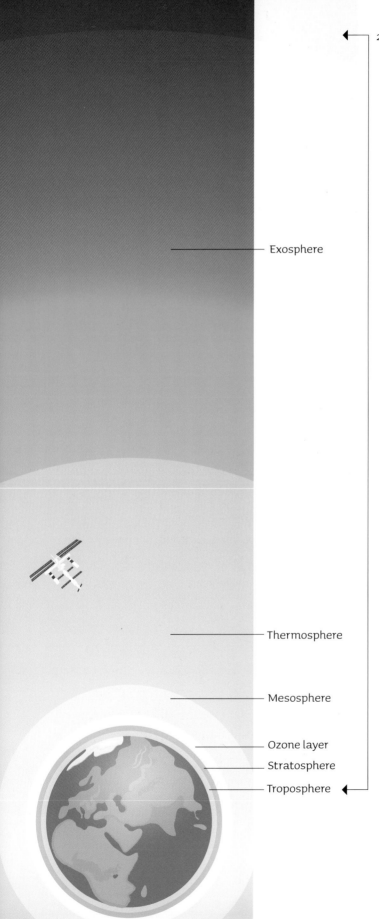

2400 kilometers

Exosphere

The Earth's Atmosphere

The atmosphere extends far into space, but life is possible only in the troposphere. That thin layer of air gives us the perfect temperature, air pressure, and mix of gases we need to live.

Thermosphere

Mesosphere

23

Ozone layer

Stratosphere

Troposphere

The amount of oxygen in the air begins to decrease even 2 or 3 kilometers (1 or 2 miles) up. Many people find it hard to breathe at those heights. Mountain climbers have to take oxygen with them to climb the highest peaks. And planes flying 10 to 15 kilometers (6 to 9 miles) up have to be specially built to provide normal air for passengers to breathe.

Just as important to Earth creatures as our custom-made blanket of air is another narrow zone just above it. This is the ozone layer. Ozone, a gas formed from oxygen, filters out much of the sun's harmful ultraviolet light before it strikes Earth. Ultraviolet light can damage genes—tiny, invisible "blueprints" inside all creatures that make an apple an apple, a butterfly a butterfly, and you, you. We inherit genes from our parents. They determine many things about us, such as what color of hair and eyes we have, how tall we are, and what shape our nose or mouth is. This thin layer of ozone is another amazing gift of the air, protecting all life on Earth.

Air Today, Gone Tomorrow?

As you have seen, animals breathe in oxygen and breathe out carbon dioxide. Plants take in carbon dioxide and release oxygen. Together, animals and plants keep our atmosphere in perfect balance. One of the great things about this system is that carbon dioxide and other gases in the air act like a blanket. After the sun's rays hit Earth, the gases keep some of the heat from escaping. This heat warms the Earth and makes life possible. Amazingly, this perfect balance of gases has lasted for hundreds of thousands of years.

But now we humans are threatening the balance. About 250 years ago, people started making things in factories. These factories burned fuels such as wood, coal, oil, and gas. When they are burned, they create carbon dioxide, which goes into the air. And in the last 100 years, cars, trucks, and planes, which also run on oil or gas, have sent even more carbon dioxide into the air. At the same time, we have destroyed a great many forests, so there are fewer trees to absorb the extra carbon dioxide. And so the blanket gets thicker.

Carbon Sinks

Forests are very effective "carbon sinks."
That means they absorb large amounts
of carbon dioxide and keep it out of the
atmosphere. But when forests are burned or
cut down, they become "carbon sources,"
releasing the stored carbon back into the air.

The result is that we have sent so much carbon dioxide into the air, especially in the last 50 years, that plants can't remove it fast enough. And scientists tell us that increased amounts of carbon dioxide are raising the Earth's air temperature. You may have heard of this global change in temperature—it's called global warming or climate change. We are already seeing some of its effects. For example, glaciers at the North Pole are melting, and more droughts and violent storms are occurring in many areas. Scientists think that sea levels may rise and other dramatic changes may happen unless we can put the brakes on our carbon dioxide emissions.

Gas Pains

Like carbon dioxide, methane is a "greenhouse gas," which holds heat
in the air like the glass walls of a greenhouse and contributes to
global warming. Methane comes mainly from human-related sources,
such as the large-scale farming of animals for food. In animals such
as cows, sheep, and goats, methane is produced during digestion
and then exhaled or expelled. The good news is that methane
can be recovered and used as fuel, called biogas.

Factories and vehicles also send harmful gases into the air that endanger the health of people, animals, and plants. If you live in a city, you have probably seen the haze of smog or smelled the fumes of air pollution. It is not pleasant! Not only that, but some of these gases have drifted up to the ozone layer and damaged parts of it. For more than 20 years there has been a large "hole" (a decrease in the amount of ozone) in the ozone layer over Antarctica. In 2008, space satellites showed the hole to be almost three times the size of Europe. This large hole means that too much ultraviolet light may be reaching Earth and harming ocean life, crops, and people.

Fixing the Hole

Scientists discovered that emissions from chemicals used to make everyday products, such as refrigerators, and sprays, such as hairspray and spray paint, were creating a hole in the ozone layer. Laws were passed to reduce the use of those chemicals, and since then the hole has stopped growing.

Fortunately, many nations are trying to stop the damage to the air. Governments are passing laws to control the gases released by factories and vehicles. New, cleaner fuels are being tested, and cars that use less fuel are being built. Forestry companies are using logging methods that keep forests alive. And many people are cutting down on their car trips by riding bikes, taking buses or other forms of public transportation, or using car pools more often. These are some of the many ways we can help keep that "air soup" we're in a healthy brew.

We don't know much about how the Earth has kept the air fit for life for so long. But we do know that we are changing it. That's mostly because we take air for granted. But when you think about it, you realize that you can't draw a line to mark where the air ends and we begin. The air is part of us. *We are the air.* If we want to keep breathing this life-giving substance, we'll have to remember that. Because whatever we do to the air, we do to ourselves.

Air Magic

You can't see the air, but this activity shows how real it is.

WHAT YOU NEED
· A clear juice glass
· A piece of stiff light cardboard about 12 cm (5 inches) square

WHAT TO DO
Do all these steps over a large sink.

1. Fill the glass half full of water.

2. Wet the rim with your finger and put the cardboard on top.

3. Press the cardboard firmly against the rim so that there is no open space. Still pressing the cardboard with one hand, turn the glass upside down with the other hand. Now carefully let go of the cardboard. Did the trick work the first time? What would happen if you turned the glass sideways before letting go?

WHAT'S GOING ON?
The water stayed in the glass because the pressure of the air in the room pushing against the cardboard was greater than the pressure of the water against the cardboard.

A Lot of Hot Air

The temperature of the air makes a big difference to how it behaves. Try this activity and you'll see some hot action.

WHAT YOU NEED

· A pencil

· A piece of thick paper (for example, a magazine cover)

· Scissors

· A piece of thin string about 30 cm (12 inches) long

SAFETY TIP: Don't test the spiral over a hot stove or any kind of flame, since the paper could catch fire.

WHAT TO DO

1. On your paper, draw a spiral about 15 cm (6 inches) across. Cut it out along the circular lines.

2. Use the scissors to poke a small hole in the center of the spiral. Knot one end of the string. Push the other end through the hole from underneath and pull it through to the knot.

3. Hold your spiral over a heater, radiator, or hot light bulb. What happens?

4. Test other spots in your home for hot air currents. Where do you find rising warm air?

WHAT'S GOING ON?
When air heats up, the molecules (groups of atoms) in it spread out and it gets lighter. Warm air rises, and cooler air falls. As the air moved, your spiral had to move too.

Dirty Air Detectors

How clean is the air you're breathing?

· Several plastic drinking glasses, well washed and dried

· Petroleum jelly

· A magnifying glass

· A notebook and pen or pencil

· The same number of large empty cans as drinking glasses, tops and bottoms removed

· Masking tape

WHAT TO DO

1. Decide where you want to test for air pollution. Choose a variety of sites, including some you think are pretty clean (maybe your room, your yard, or a park), some you think are dirty (near a highway, in a factory yard), and some in between (beside a road).

2. Smear the outside of one of the glasses with petroleum jelly and examine it with your magnifying glass. In your notebook, write down what you see. You need to know what a clean glass looks like so that you can compare your findings with it later.

3. Put the glass at your first test spot. Label it with a piece of masking tape stuck to the inside. Cover the glass with a can. The can will keep out most dust from the ground that would confuse the results. Now you have your first detector.

4. Make the rest of your detectors and put them at your test sites. Be sure to label each detector with the name of the site. Try to find spots where they'll be protected from rain. (Rain could wash away the evidence.)

5. Check the detectors every day for a week and record any changes in your notebook.

6. Collect the detectors at the end of the week and examine them carefully with your magnifying glass. Do you see much difference between the glasses? Have you caught any strange-looking particles or specks? Are there any surprises?

7. Here's a rough pollution guide: Mark a 0.5-cm (¼-inch) square on each collector and count the number of particles you see. If there are around 15, the site is probably fairly clean. But if there are 100 or more, try not to breathe too deeply in that area!

2 WELCOME TO PLANET WATER

IF YOU PLAY lots of sports and have strong muscles, you probably think you are rock solid, right? Well, you're not. You are actually a big blob of water, with just enough solid material to keep you from dribbling away onto the floor!

That's right. You're about 70 percent water. Most is inside your body's cells, the microscopic building blocks that your body is made up of. Cells are largely water. Each cell is enclosed by a thin membrane that keeps the water in. The rest of the water flows around outside the cells in various body fluids.

The Earth is mostly water, too. About 74 percent of the planet's surface is covered by water, including oceans, lakes, rivers, and polar ice caps. Even the air is filled with water vapor, which condenses, or turns to liquid, forming clouds. We are truly water creatures living on a water planet.

33

What Water Can Do

So what *is* water, exactly? You probably know that sometimes it is liquid and sometimes it is solid, when it freezes into ice. And if you boil it in a kettle, it will turn into water vapor, which is a gas. Since you see those things every day, you might think water is ho-hum stuff. But if you could look at water really, really closely, you'd find that the water molecule—the smallest part that can still be called water—is downright strange.

Molecules are made up of atoms (remember them?) that have electrical charges. Unlike most molecules, the water molecule has negative charges on one side and positive charges on the other side. As a result, it acts as a tiny magnet, attracting other molecules to stick to it. Water molecules stick to each other, and they stick to other kinds of molecules.

Water has many especially useful features. Because water molecules are attracted to other types of molecules, water can dissolve many minerals (such as salt and rock) and organic materials (such as soil). That's why it is better to wash your clothes in water than in, say, vinegar.

Blue Earth

Earth has so much water on it that it's sometimes called the blue planet.

34

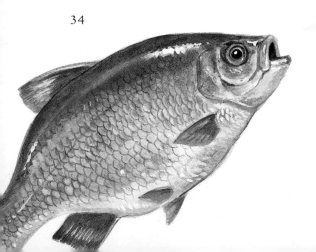

A water molecule

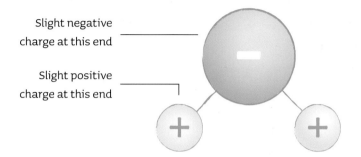

Slight negative charge at this end

Slight positive charge at this end

Weird Water

Water molecules have positive and negative charges on opposite sides. For this reason, the molecules easily bond together—the negative sides pull toward the positive sides of other molecules.

A group of water molecules bonding together

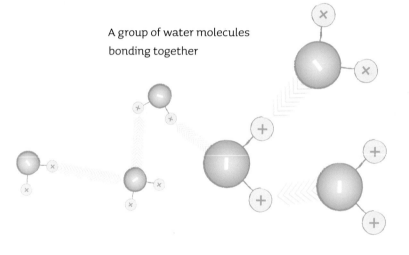

A group of water molecules being heated

A group of other molecules being heated

Low temperature

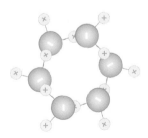

High temperature

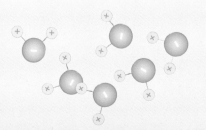

Water Alert!

Here's what happens when your body gets too little water.

1. Body fluids get saltier, containing less water and/or more salt.

2. Saltier body fluids send message to pituitary gland.

3. Message sent to kidneys: "Hold the urine!"

4. Amount of blood in heart is reduced, telling thirst center to release less saliva.

5. Mouth gets dry—you feel thirsty.

Here's what happens when your body gets too much water—the process works in reverse.

1. Body fluids get less salty and/or more watery.

2. Watery body fluids send message to pituitary gland.

3. Message sent to kidneys: "Release more urine!"

4. Bladder releases lots of watery urine.

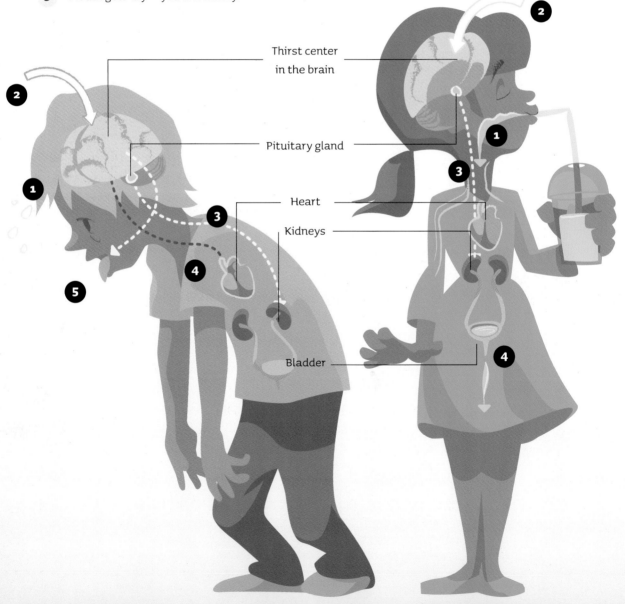

Thirst center in the brain

Pituitary gland

Heart

Kidneys

Bladder

But most useful of all, water can store large amounts of heat and then release it slowly into the air. Because water molecules easily bond to each other, water is very stable. The molecules in other liquid substances are easily disturbed by heating and soon fly off as gases. But it takes a lot more heat to change liquid water to water vapor. For this reason, the oceans can absorb heat in summer and release it in winter. The oceans can also absorb heat in the tropics and release the heat in northern areas. So the ability of water to store heat and to move as a liquid affects weather patterns all over the Earth.

Why You Drink All That Milk, Juice, and Pop

You know that cotton-ball feeling your mouth gets on a hot summer day, especially when you've been playing hard? That's your body yelling, "Give me water!" If you were lost in a desert without any water, you wouldn't last more than a few days. Next to air, water is your body's most important need.

Your body is a perpetual water recycler. It constantly uses up water in processes such as digestion and releases it in your breath, sweat, tears, urine, and feces. So you have to keep supplying your body with water—about 1.5 to 2 liters (quarts) a day, depending on how hot it is and how active you are. You get this amount of water from both food and drinks. But the amount of water that goes into your body and the amount that goes out have to be exactly the same, or you're in trouble. Fortunately, unless the situation gets really drastic, your body's inner alarm system will keep the water balance stable.

Water also helps regulate your body's temperature. Did you know that you sweat to cool off? When it is hot, sweat comes

Rain-Forest Recycling

Each tree in the Amazon Basin—
the largest area of rain forest on Earth—
can send 700 tonnes of water into
the air a year, creating clouds and
affecting weather over a wide area.

out of tiny pores all over your skin. The sweat then evaporates, or changes from a liquid to water vapor. Evaporation takes heat, and that heat is pulled from your body. Try licking your hand and blowing on it to make the moisture evaporate. See how cool your skin feels?

How Water Gets Around

After your sweat goes into the air, what do you suppose happens to it? Well, in a few months the moisture might turn up in a drenching rainstorm or a snowstorm or land in the ocean. Or if a molecule of your sweat fell on the ground, it might get slurped up by a tree rootlet, travel all the way to a leaf, and be released into the air from there. That's because you don't just recycle your body's water. You are part of a much larger, grander show— the Earth's great water cycle.

Earth's Water Dance

Water is always on the move. Water from your sweat and from oceans and rivers evaporates into the atmosphere. Some of that water forms clouds. Then rain or snow falls, soaking into the ground and filling up rivers and oceans. Some water in the ground is drawn up by plant rootlets, where it makes its way to leaves, and from there goes back into the atmosphere.

Clouds condense.

Rain or snow falls onto land.

Water returns to the atmosphere.

Energy from the sun causes water to evaporate.

Water seeps into the ground.

Water runs into streams.

Ocean

Ahaiyuta and the Cloud-Eater

This story is told by the Zuñi people, who have lived for many centuries in the hot deserts of New Mexico.

Long, long ago, on top of a great mountain to the east, lived the monster Cloud-Eater. He'd always had a big appetite for clouds, but for months now he had been in a cloud-eating frenzy, snatching each one that rolled by with his huge, gaping mouth. Without clouds, there had been no rain, and the land was dry and baked hard. The cornstalks shriveled in the fields, and the people and their animals were starving.

Far in the west, young Ahaiyuta lived with his grandmother. He was brave and strong, like his father, the Sun. "I must go to the mountain and slay Cloud-Eater," Ahaiyuta said one day. "Then the rains will come, and the people will be happy."

"Be careful!" warned his grandmother. "Cloud-Eater has fought off many fine warriors who tried to kill him. Take these four feathers to help you. But guard them carefully, for they are very powerful. The red feather will lead the way. The blue feather will let you talk with the animals. The yellow feather will make you as small as the tiniest creatures, and the black feather will give you strength for your task."

Ahaiyuta stuck the red feather in his hair, thanked his grandmother, and set off on his long journey. As he walked along, a blazing sun beat down on him, and he began to feel thirsty, hungry, and tired. Not a creature stirred.

Suddenly, he saw a gopher standing beside its hole. Ahaiyuta stuck the blue and yellow feathers in his hair. In a flash he was the gopher's size.

"Gracious!" said the gopher. "That was an excellent trick! But where are you going in this terrible heat?" Ahaiyuta told the gopher what he had come to do.

"I will help you," said the gopher. "My home has an underground passage leading right to Cloud-Eater's mountain. I will take you to him."

Ahaiyuta followed the gopher into its hole. They ran swiftly along the tunnel, which took a steep climb as they reached the mountain. At last they could hear the monster snoring just above them. The gopher scampered ahead, tunneling through the dirt until he broke through to where the monster was lying. He began to gnaw the fur that covered the monster's heart.

"Whazzat?" the monster mumbled sleepily.

"Don't worry, Grandfather," the gopher replied. "I'm just taking a few hairs to line my nest. You'll never miss them."

The gopher ran to Ahaiyuta and told him what he had done. "The tunnel leads to Cloud-Eater's heart," he said. "Aim well—and good luck!"

Ahaiyuta put the black feather in his hair and crept along the tunnel until he saw his target. He placed an arrow in his bow, aimed carefully, and then—strike! Immediately great roars and shrieks filled the air. The Earth shook and rocks tumbled as Cloud-Eater thrashed about in his bed. Finally, all was still.

"Cloud-Eater has eaten his last cloud!" cried Ahaiyuta. "Now it will rain."

The gopher and Ahaiyuta ran back through the tunnel to the entrance. When they emerged, dark clouds already covered the Sun, and large drops of rain were beginning to fall. Soon rain was pouring from the sky, soaking the earth with its nourishing gifts. Ahaiyuta thanked the gopher and waved good-bye. As streams of water swirled about his feet, he laughed with delight and began to run. He knew that he had saved his people.

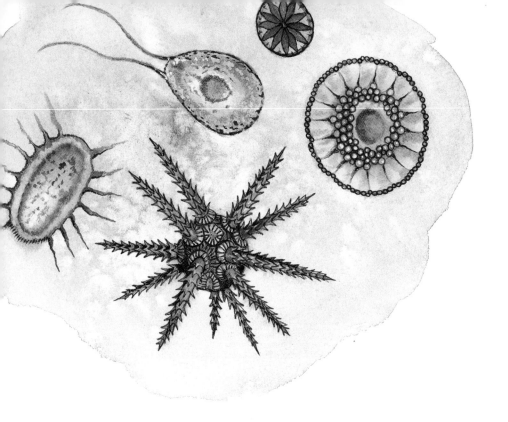

How Water Learned to Dance

Water has not always existed on Earth. It developed gradually
over hundreds of millions of years. In the very beginning, Earth
was a fiery planet—so hot that water couldn't have existed in a
liquid form. It would have all turned to water vapor after being
blown up into the air from volcanoes.

A few million years later, though, when the world had cooled
down a bit, water vapor began to form clouds. Eventually this
water vapor fell as rain. After a few more million years, rain was
pouring down onto a landscape of rocky mountains and deep
valleys. After many more millions of years, fresh water covered
most of the Earth. It began to dissolve and wash away mineral
salts in the rock. Finally, large seas of salty water were created.

Then, more than 3 billion years ago, the first life-forms—
very simple, bacteria-like organisms—appeared in the oceans.
And now that life was here, the great water dance could begin.

Life Needs Fresh Water

If you've ever swallowed a mouthful of ocean water by mistake, you know how salty it is. And that's where more than 97 percent of the Earth's water is—in the oceans. What humans and most other animals and plants need to survive, though, is unsalty water, or fresh water. We need it for drinking, washing, and irrigating our food crops. One of the marvels of the water cycle is that it changes salty water from the oceans into the fresh water we need. When the sun's rays heat the oceans, water vapor rises into the sky, leaving the salt behind. Then water vapor falls back to Earth as rain or snow, refilling the streams and soaking deep into the ground.

Rain constantly renews the Earth's supply of fresh water. But that does not mean the supply is endless. Most of the Earth's freshwater stores are frozen in glaciers or buried deep underground. Compared with all the water on Earth, the amount of drinking water we can get to—in rivers, lakes, and wells—is very small.

Moon Aliens?

Life on Earth started in the water, so scientists looking for life in space look for water first. So far, the best evidence of liquid water on any body outside Earth is in pictures taken by the spacecraft *Cassini* in 2002. They show spouting geysers on Enceladus, a moon of the planet Saturn.

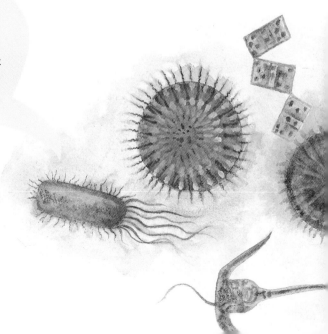

Drop in a Bucket

The Earth has plenty of water—but
most of it is in the salty oceans, in
glaciers, or buried deep underground.
The teaspoon in the picture below
represents the amountof fresh water
we can get at and use.

Total amount of
water on Earth

Total amount of
fresh water on Earth

Total amount of
fresh water available

Supplies of fresh water vary enormously in different parts of the world. Canada is lucky to have a large amount in its many rivers and lakes, though much of it is too far north to be accessible. In many other countries, fresh water is scarce. The central part of Australia, for example, is mostly a desert. As a result, almost all of the people in Australia live along the country's south coast. Fresh, clean water is scarcest in the countries of the developing world. Today, water shortages plague almost all of the countries of North Africa and the Middle East.

Water Down the Drain

No creature is as clever as humans at finding ways to capture, move, store, and especially use water. In the United States and Canada, people use vast amounts of water in their homes for drinking, cooking, cleaning, and watering their lawns. And factories use even more water to make all of the things we buy. They use water, for instance, to generate electricity, mix chemicals, wash away waste materials, and transport wood fiber in pulp.

Think about dinnertime at your place. Perhaps you drink a glass of water with your meal. There's also the water used to grow your vegetables and the water power that may be used to generate the electricity that turns on your lights. Then there's the water used by the factories that made your dishes, knives and forks, tablecloth, and table. And don't forget washing the dishes—and the factories that made the dish detergent and its plastic bottle.

Besides using and wasting so much of our precious fresh water, we also pollute it. We use our oceans, lakes, and rivers

Counting the Sea Creatures

Scientists from 82 countries have been counting how many kinds of sea creatures there are and how many of each kind, mapping their movements, and tracing their history. Over 10 years, researchers have made many startling finds—strange beings deep under the Antarctic ice, such as octopuses that don't squirt ink (it's dark down below, so ink doesn't help them), and a whole ecosystem of tiny animals that live in Arctic sea ice. The Mid-Atlantic Ridge, the largest mountain range in the world and almost all under water, is crammed with creatures, many new to science.

as sewers, dumping human, farm, and factory waste into them. We build huge dams and canals so that ships can sail in from all over the world. We cut down forests lining the shores of rivers and lakes and build cities there. All these actions can pollute water and harm the health of people, other animals, plants, and entire ecosystems.

An ecosystem is a community of plants, animals, soil, and water—all interacting and depending on each other to survive in a certain place, such as a lake or prairie. If too much waste is poured into a lake, the water can become unsafe for people to drink. It can kill fish or give them diseases that make them unfit to eat. Human activities, such as building dams and cutting down forests, can destroy ecosystems that plants and animals had depended on for water, nesting places, and food.

Now we are facing a possible global water crisis. One-third of the people in the world already live where there is not enough water. That fraction may rise, since populations are growing and our water use is growing even faster.

How Laura and Losero Use Water

Losero

Losero lives in a village in Kenya. Here's how he might use water in a day.

- Drink mug of tea for breakfast.
- Take drink of water from well at school.
- After school, fill water trough for family's cattle.
- Wash hands before main meal of the day.
- Drink glass of water after meal.

Laura

Laura lives in Buffalo, New York. Here's how she might use water on a typical day.

- Brush teeth.
- Flush toilet (several times).
- Wash hands and face in sink.
- At school, clean up after art class.
- Drink from water fountain (three times).
- Wash hands before lunch.
- Fill hamster's water bottle in science class.
- Drink bottle of water after gym class.
- Go swimming after school.
- Shower after swim.
- Help Dad wash the car.
- Wash hands before dinner.
- Refill dog's water dish.
- Brush teeth.
- Take hot bath.

Water use varies greatly from country to country. Americans and Canadians each use an average of up to 1000 L (quarts) of water every day. In Kenya, many people get by on only 5 L a day.

People in North America, especially, use water as if it will never run out. But the first North Americans—the Aboriginal people, who had lived here for thousands of years when the Europeans arrived—thought of water as sacred. The great waterways provided food, water, and transportation. They were precious gifts to be respected and treated with care. These peoples believed that the oceans, rivers, and streams were part of them and that they needed them to survive.

And you know something? They were right. Not only do we need water, *we are water.* Water fills our bodies, is used in body processes such as digestion, and constantly passes through us as part of the Earth's great water cycle. Water is a precious gift we must care for if we care for ourselves.

Up, Up, and Away!

Water is the Earth's great shape-shifter. It can be a liquid, a solid (ice), or a gas (water vapor). What things help it evaporate (change from a liquid to a gas)? All it takes is . . . Well, you find out.

WHAT YOU NEED

· Measuring spoons

· 2 saucers

· 2 dish towels

· A hair dryer

· A plate

· A small bottle

WHAT TO DO

1. Put 25 mL (2 tablespoons) of water into each saucer. Put 1 saucer outside in the sun. Put the other saucer in the shade. Which saucer of water evaporates faster? Why?

2. Pour 25 mL (2 tablespoons) of water into the middle of each dish towel. Spread 1 towel out on a table. Hold the other one up in the air. Turn the hair dryer dial to "cool" and blow air on the towel. Which towel dries first? Why?

3. Now measure 25 mL (2 tablespoons) of water onto the plate. Put the same amount into the small bottle. Place them somewhere side by side for a few hours. This time, which container of water evaporates first? Why?

WHAT'S GOING ON?

Water evaporates faster when it is heated, when wind blows across it, and when it is not very deep. When water is heated, the molecules pull apart and jump around. They fly off into the surrounding air as a gas, taking heat with them. Wind speeds up the process. Spreading water out helps, too. The molecules are closer to the surface and can fly off more easily.

49

A Solar Pure-Water Still

This mini version of the Earth's water cycle makes clean (purified) water from muddy water. Called a still, it uses the same natural methods as the water cycle—evaporation and condensation—to make clean water in a dishpan.

WHAT YOU NEED
· Water

· A large dishpan

· Garden soil

· A drinking glass shorter than the sides of the pan

· Some clean marbles

· Plastic wrap wider than the pan

· Masking tape

WHAT TO DO
1. To make muddy water, put about 5 cm (2 inches) of water in the dishpan. Add a little garden soil and stir it around.

2. To make the still, set the glass in the middle of the dishpan. If the glass moves around, put a few marbles in it to weigh it down.

3. Moisten the rim of the dishpan so that you can make a tight seal. Fit a piece of plastic wrap over the dishpan. Pull it smooth, but leave a tiny bit of slack. (You might want some help with this step.) Attach the plastic securely with masking tape.

4. Place a marble in the center of the plastic, directly over the glass. You want the plastic to dip down but not touch the glass.

5. Put your still outside in direct sunlight. Leave it for several hours and watch what happens.

WHAT'S GOING ON?
The heat of the sun begins to turn the water into water vapor. The vapor rises, leaving the dirt behind. When the vapor hits the plastic, it cools because the air outside is cooler than the air inside. (Just like the glass roof on a greenhouse, the plastic has trapped heat inside the pan.) The water vapor condenses back into a liquid, which falls into the glass like rain. You now have clean, "distilled" water.

Toilets 'n' Taps

These activities are gross in a way, but maybe not the way you think. It's all about the water we waste—in toilets, showers, sinks, and other places around our homes.

WHAT YOU NEED
· A heavy, narrow, waterproof object (for example, a plastic jug weighed down with sand or rocks)
· A large cooking pot
· A measuring cup
· A bucket
· A notebook and pen or pencil
· A watch with a second hand

WHAT TO DO
Put a jug in it!

1. Lift the cover off the toilet tank (or ask an adult to do it). Flush the toilet and watch how it works. Each flush uses about 20 L (5 gallons) of water. That's more than you usually need for a flush.

2. Put a heavy object in the tank (without disturbing the mechanism). It will save a lot of wasted water. The object takes up space, so less water is needed to fill the tank.

Brush off!

1. Do you brush your teeth with the water running? Try this. Put the pot in the sink and turn on the cold water.

Pretend to brush your teeth as the water runs into the pot. When you finish, turn off the tap.

2. Measure the water in the pot with your measuring cup. (Pour each cupful into the bucket. Use the water to flush the toilet or water plants.)

3. Write down how much water you used. Could you do the job with less?

Leakin' lizards!

1. Check every tap in your home for leaks. If you find one, tighten the handle to see if it stops. If not, put it on a list to get fixed.

2. Try this test: Put your measuring cup under a tap and turn it on so that it drips. Time how long it takes to fill the cup. Multiply that by 4 to get how long it takes to drip 1 L (1 quart). A bath can use 100 L (26 gallons) of water. How long would it take that leak to fill a bathtub?

WHAT'S GOING ON?
It's easy to waste water, but it's easy *not* to waste it, too. You can do a perfectly good job of brushing your teeth by turning the tap on and off or rinsing with a glass of water. You can have a fine shower under a water-saving showerhead that cuts water use by half. And if you get leaky taps fixed, you won't notice any difference at all— except that maddening *drip-drip* will be gone!

3 GETTING DOWN TO EARTH

THREE-QUARTERS OF THE planet may be covered by water, but you and I live on good old, solid—you know, the stuff our planet is named for. Earth, soil, ground, land—whatever you call it, it's as common as, well, dirt.

When you were a little kid, didn't you love digging in the dirt and making mud pies? You might even have tried a taste. But now you'd probably rather grab a slice of pizza or scarf down a hunk of chocolate cake with thick, gooey frosting. Did you know that both that cake and the pizza came from dirt? In fact, just about everything you eat comes from the soil.

Dining on Dirt

Say you had a ham sandwich, an apple, and milk for lunch one day. Here's how the whole thing came from the soil.

Cow

Bread

Pig

Apple

Mustard

Salt

Flour

Lettuce

Corn

Fuel up

As you can see, every bit of this lunch not only came from dirt but was once a living plant or animal. (Okay, all except the salt, which is a mineral.) The same is true of all the food you eat. You are basically a compost heap for dead things! After you put that food in your mouth, your body does a wonderful job of grinding and mixing and mushing it all up into a gloppy soup. And that gets broken down further into nutrients the body needs for life itself.

The most important of these nutrients are fats, proteins, and carbohydrates. To be healthy, you need to get enough of them, together with water, fiber, and certain vitamins and minerals, every day. Luckily, most foods you eat contain several of these nutrients. A peanut butter sandwich on whole wheat bread, for example, contains most of them. So it's easier to choose a healthy diet if you think of foods rather than nutrients.

The Top Four

Scientists have divided foods into four groups according to the nutrients they contain. The daily amounts given here are for kids aged 9 to 13.

1 MEAT & ALTERNATIVES
(1–2 servings)

2 MILK PRODUCTS
(3–4 servings)

3 VEGETABLES & FRUITS
(6 servings)

4 GRAIN PRODUCTS
(6 servings)

Gulp!

How a bowl of chili gives you great hair

1   Nose smells chili.

2   Salivary glands release saliva. Saliva moistens food.

3   Teeth chew food into softened lumps.

4   Tongue sends lumps of food down throat.

5   Food moves from esophagus to stomach.

6   Digestive juices break down fats and proteins.

7   Liquid food passes into small intestine, which breaks down carbohydrates and absorbs nutrients and water.

8   Food not absorbed into body passes into large intestine.

9   Large intestine releases remaining food products from body.

10 Absorbed nutrients pass into your blood and are carried to all parts of your body, including your hair.

Where Dirt Came From

How far down does the ground go? Do you think it goes right to the center of the Earth? Actually, it's a very thin layer. If the Earth were a giant tomato, 70 meters (77 yards) around the middle, the soil would be far thinner than the tomato's skin. Below that thin layer is solid rock and hot liquid rock.

That skinny covering coat of soil wasn't always here. Like air and water, soil developed gradually over billions of years. Let's get back into our timeship and find out how that happened.

Okay, we're back in the early days of the Earth, when hot melted rock was beginning to cool and harden into solid rock. It's a good thing we have our heat-proof suits on, because it's still fiery hot. But there is no soil anywhere, so let's not hang around here. In a few million years, things are going to get a lot more interesting, not to mention more comfortable.

Now it's hundreds of millions of years later, and we can see how wind, rain, and snow have begun to break down the rock. The smaller chunks are being moved across the surface of the Earth by wind, glaciers, gravity, and running water. And as they move, the chunks are getting smaller. This process is called weathering. And, amazingly, over many millions of years, weathering can wear down mountains and turn boulders into sand.

Back in our timeship now, we'll zoom ahead to about 3.5 billion years ago and have a look at one of the oceans. Our ship, of course, is totally seaworthy and can sail to the bottom like a submarine. Look—the ocean floor is covered in fine silt. This silt was created when water on land weathered certain types of rock into powdery bits and washed them out to sea. And the first tiny life-forms have been born in the ocean brew.

Some are making their way onto land. Masses of those microorganisms are invading cracks in the rock, looking for nutrients. That pressure is breaking down the rock, too. On land there is now sand, clay, dust, and gravel, but still no soil.

We take another big jump ahead in our timeship, to 350 million years ago. Now plants have moved out of the oceans. Together with bacteria, they are really going to town on the rocks. To anchor themselves, plants have sent their roots deep into any holes they can find, crumbling the rock. Bacteria have released chemicals that have dissolved rock and produced nutrients they could use. And what's this over here? Zillions of bacteria and plants have died over the years, and their bodies have mixed in with the powdered rock. A little mound of brown crumbly stuff has formed. The breakdown of life-forms has finally created soil.

Let's zoom ahead a few more million years. As dead matter and broken-down rocks and minerals have piled up, the soil has in many places become richer and deeper. Over time, larger plants like trees and bigger animals have died and added their bodies to the soil. Their bodies have enriched the soil just as the soil nourished them.

Time to go home now to the present. We'll take a quick trip around our planet. (Conveniently, our timeship is also a spaceship.) As we speed around the globe, we see a fantastic variety of plants, trees, mammals, insects, birds, and other creatures forming a multitude of different communities—prairie

The Myth of Gaia

The early Greeks told this story to show how important soil is.

GAIA WAS the great mother-goddess of the Earth, the provider and creator of all things. She created Uranus, god of the heavens, and together they peopled the universe. She made the storm-spirits and other forces of nature, as well as human beings.

One of Gaia's granddaughters was Demeter, who later took on some of the Earth Mother's role as the goddess of planted soil, fertility, and the harvest. Demeter had a daughter, Persephone. One day, as Persephone was gathering flowers in a sunlit field, she was kidnapped by her uncle Hades, king of the underworld. Hades' kingdom was the fearful home of the dead, but it was also the source of life and growth. When Persephone disappeared underground, all growth stopped on Earth.

Demeter searched all over the world for her lost daughter. Finally Hades agreed to return her to her mother so that harvests could begin again. But unknown to Persephone, the gods had proclaimed that if she ate any food in the underworld, she would have to remain there forever. To keep her with him, cunning Hades offered her a seed of the pomegranate as a parting gift. Persephone ate it and so was ordered to return to Hades' realm for part of every year. But in the spring she could return again, bringing new life to the Earth.

Ever since that time, leaves and plants have returned to the dark soil to bloom again in spring. Each year the world must die to be reborn again from the Earth, the mother of us all.

> "Dakota children understand that we are of the soil and the soil of us, that we have the birds and beasts that grew with us on this soil. A bond exists between all things because they all drink the same water and breathe the same air."
>
> LUTHER STANDING BEAR, *My People the Sioux*

Sacred Soil

Soil directly supplies 98 percent of the world's food. Even though fish is a staple in the diet of many cultures, most people in the world live primarily on three grasses—rice, corn, and wheat. Humans have depended on plants and soil for food since we first appeared on Earth.

The early peoples thought of the Earth—both planet and soil—as sacred. Earth was home and the provider of life. Since the Earth cared for them, they respected and cared for the Earth. Aboriginal people still have this idea today. They often refer to Earth as "Mother Earth" because it gives birth to all life.

But most of the world has a different view. Rather than honoring the Earth, we often destroy it. The Earth's precious topsoil—the thin, fertile upper layer—was formed over thousands of years as generations of plants and animals died and enriched it with nutrients from their bodies. But now the world's supply of topsoil is shrinking. Although nature creates new fertile soil every year, we destroy 23 billion tonnes more than is made. We do this by cutting down forests and allowing the soil underneath to be swept away by wind and rain. We do it by paving over more and more of our best farmland to put up

buildings and parking lots. Mostly we do it by
using harmful farming methods.

Most of the food you eat comes from huge farms where
the goal is to produce bigger and bigger crops as fast as
possible. To achieve this aim, farmers douse their fields
with powerful chemical fertilizers and pesticides. The
chemicals in these products pollute the air, the ground, and
any nearby water. They also kill many of the soil microorganisms that create new soil. Farmers on these factory-like
farms often plant the same crop over and over, not allowing
enough time between plantings for soil to become fertile again
naturally. At the same time, the world's population is growing by about 80 million people a year, so even more fertile soil
is needed to grow food. To meet that need, forests are being
rapidly cut down and the soil used for planting crops. Cutting
down trees for farmland is a major cause of forest loss
throughout the world.

But many people are concerned about what's happening
to the soil. Organic farming is one answer that has become
very popular. Many grocery stores sell organic fruits and vegetables now. Organic farmers try to use nature's own methods
to grow food and keep soil healthy. For example, they fertilize
the soil with compost (dead plants) and plant a variety of crops.
They keep the soil rich in nutrients by planting different crops
from season to season. And they don't use chemical pesticides.

Instead, they use bacteria that kill crop-eating insects without harming other animals. Figuring out how nature does things is not easy, since every area has its own ecosystem, in which soil, weather, plants, and animals are related to each other in a very complex way. But it's worth the effort.

HAVE YOU heard the expression "You are what you eat"? It is scientifically true. And since almost everything you eat comes from the soil, it's also true that just as you are air and water, *you are also the Earth.* That's a good reason to honor it and treat it well.

Disappearing Forests

In the last 200 years, the Earth has lost two-thirds of its forests as a result of human activities. Today the net loss increases each year by an area the size of Panama— 75,517 km² (29,157 square miles).

Journey Under the Earth

Let's go underground—half a meter (20 inches) below the surface of the soil. That might not seem like much, but you will discover that things are very different down under.

WHAT YOU NEED
· A small shovel or trowel
· Topsoil from a garden
· 2 large plastic containers
· Subsoil from about 50 cm (20 inches) down in the ground
· Newspapers
· A magnifying glass
· 2 small empty cans
· 2 bean seeds

WHAT TO DO
1. Collect a scoopful of garden soil and put it into one of the plastic containers. (Get permission before digging.)

2. A good place to get subsoil is from a bank or ditch where the soil has been cut or worn away. Or you can dig a hole in your garden. (Again, get permission first.) Put a scoopful of subsoil into the second container.

3. Spread newspapers on a flat surface and carefully examine your 2 samples with your magnifying glass. How are the soils different? Which do you think would be better for growing plants in?

4. Now fill 1 can with topsoil and the other with subsoil. Soak the bean seeds in water overnight and then plant one in each can. Water both cans lightly and put them in a sunny spot. Keep the soils moist. Watch the plants for several days. Which plant is stronger? Was your prediction right?

WHAT'S GOING ON?
Subsoil contains more stones and less humus, or organic matter (dead leaves, roots, twigs, and soil-dwelling animals), than topsoil. So it isn't very good for growing plants. Topsoil contains what plants need to thrive—organic matter and microscopic organisms such as bacteria to break it down.

65

Fake Fossils

Fossils are traces of plants or animals left in the Earth's crust millions of years ago. Most fossils are petrified (turned to stone) or are imprints found in rock. Real fossils take thousands of years to form, but you can make fake versions in a few minutes.

RAISE YOUR PAWS

WHAT YOU NEED

· Tape

· A piece of cardboard about 10 cm x 30 cm (4 inches x 12 inches)

· Plaster of Paris

· A plastic container

· A jar of water

· A stirring stick or spoon

WHAT TO DO

1. Go for a hike with your materials in a backpack. Look for animal footprints where there is soft, damp soil, such as near a riverbank or along a forest path after it has rained.

2. When you find a clear print, gently brush away any leaves, stones, or loose dirt. Tape the cardboard strip into a ring. Center it over the print and push it firmly into the soil.

3. Stir a little plaster of Paris into the container. Slowly stir in water until you have a soft, thick mixture something like toothpaste. Spoon it out over the print to a depth of about 3 cm (a little over an inch) and smooth it. Let it harden—about half an hour.

4. Carefully lift the mold. You will have a raised impression of the footprint for your fossil collection.

5. Be sure to take all your materials home with you.

SUNKEN GARDEN

SAFETY TIP: Ask an adult to help you bake the fossil.

WHAT YOU NEED

· Modeling clay

· A rolling pin

· Leaves, flowers, or other natural items to "fossilize"

· A table knife

· Optional: food coloring

WHAT TO DO

1. If you want a colored print, mix food coloring into the clay first. Then roll out a chunk of clay until it's about 2 cm (¾ inch) thick.

2. Center a leaf or other item, vein side down, on the clay. Press it firmly into the clay with the rolling pin. Carefully remove the leaf. You might want to cut off the edges of the clay to make a circle, square, or other shape. Use the same method to make as many prints as you like.

3. Bake your fossil in the oven, at the lowest temperature, until it hardens—1 or 2 hours.

Supermarket Sleuth

Do you know what you are eating? Pick 3 or 4 foods you'd like to find out about. If you choose a food in a can or box, read the fine print and list all the ingredients in a notebook. Write down the country where the food came from. Research all the ingredients, using books or the Internet. Try to find out what they are and why they are in the food—such as to make it stay fresh longer.

Another Idea...

If you have a blog (short for weblog), or your class has one, you could post photos of your fossils on it. You might want to set up a regular nature section in the blog to write about your discoveries.

4 FIRE POWER

DO YOU LOVE summer? You probably get a burst of energy as soon as the sun tells you it's T-shirt time. But the sun gives you a lot more than just great weather to play in outside. Every bit of energy that makes life possible on Earth—from coal-burning furnaces and water-powered electricity right down to your ability to hit a home run—comes from the sun.

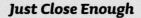

Just Close Enough

The Earth is 150 million kilometers (93 million miles) from the sun. That is a perfect distance, as it makes our planet neither too hot nor too cold for life to begin. The distance seems far, but the sun's energy takes only 8.5 minutes to get here.

Plugging into the Sun

What is energy? Scientists describe it as the ability to do work. And work means any kind of activity. Scientists have learned that energy can't be created out of nothing; it has to be obtained from something else.

For example, suppose you want to hammer a nail into a piece of wood. The energy you need to do that comes from energy stored in your body. That energy comes from the food you've eaten. (Remember the chili picture?) All your food came from plants (and from animals that eat plants), and the energy in the plants came from the sun. Plants receive light and heat energy from the sun through radiation—invisible rays that travel through the air to Earth. If you have ever grown vegetables in a garden or flowers in a window box, you know that plants need sunlight to grow.

It is thanks to plants, in fact, that we are able to use the sun's energy at all. Billions of years ago, the microscopic ancestors of plants learned to absorb sunlight and, together with water and carbon dioxide, change it into food. This process of photosynthesis was a giant breakthrough in evolution because it made the sun's vast, endless supply of energy accessible to evolving life-forms. Ever since, all life has been able to use this energy by eating plants. All the energy in our bodies is actually sunlight captured by plants.

But back to the nail. When you hit the nail, the energy is transferred to it in the form of motion (the nail goes into the wood) and heat. You can feel the warmth in the nail for a second or two. Then the heat spreads out into the wood and air. Although it isn't lost, it is no longer available to do work—it has decayed. Energy in the world is always decaying like that. Fortunately, the sun constantly floods the Earth with more energy to recharge its batteries.

All living things need the sun's energy. Plants and animals need energy to grow and reproduce. You need energy to move, to see, to breathe. You need a little energy just to lie in the grass, thinking deep thoughts. Even when you're sleeping, your body is giving off as much heat as a 100-watt light bulb.

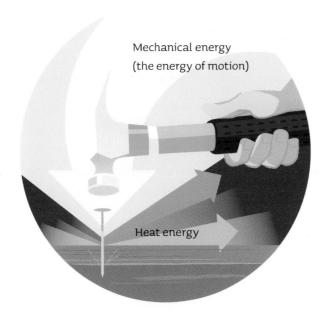

Mechanical energy
(the energy of motion)

Heat energy

When you hammer a nail into a block of wood, you're using "mechanical" energy (muscle power). After you hit the nail, that energy changes to heat energy, which goes into the nail, wood, and air.

Your Perfect Inner Furnace

Have you ever shivered with cold on a frosty morning or sweltered in the heat of a summer afternoon? As miserable as the outer you—toes, fingers, skin—might have felt, the deepest part of your body was a comfortable 37°C (98°F) the whole time. That's because your body-core temperature stays about the same, whatever the outside temperature may be. This constant inner temperature keeps your body's engines—blood circulation, breathing, digestion, and so on—humming along smoothly.

Your body has three main ways of keeping the inner you nice and toasty.

The first is metabolism, the body's main source of heat. Metabolism is the process that breaks down nutrients such as fats, carbohydrates, and proteins into simpler materials, releasing energy for the body's work. Besides keeping you warm, this energy is used for growth and the repair of body cells and tissues.

Your body's second source of heat is your skin, which absorbs heat. You lose heat through your skin, too. If the air is cold, you can lose up to one-third of your body heat through exposed skin.

Your third source of body heat is muscle activity. As you know, playing hockey or soccer on a cold day warms you up, while too much running around on a hot day makes you feel even hotter. Up to 90 percent of your body heat can come from moving your muscles.

When it's really cold outside, you might stomp your feet and wave your arms about. And something else happens—you shiver. That's a kind of muscular activity, too. Receptors in your skin sense the cold air and send signals to the "shivering center" in your brain. It tells your muscles to move, creating heat.

Taking the Heat

Your skin is a natural "heat-protector suit," helping to keep the inner you at just the right temperature. Skin absorbs heat through the flow of air or water over it, from radiating sources such as the sun or fire, and through contact with hot things.

Flow of hot water
over skin

Direct contact
with a hot surface

A radiating source

Your brain also relays the message to tiny muscles inside your blood vessels, telling them to shrink. That cuts down the blood flow to your skin, hands, and feet and keeps it where it counts most—in your inner core. You have tiny muscles at the base of your hair roots that react the same way, and then *brrrr*—goose bumps.

If you're too hot, blood vessels near your skin expand. That increases the blood flow from your center to your skin, and the blood brings heat with it. Your skin becomes flushed, and then you sweat. Water is released through special sweat glands—you have about 2.5 million of them all over your skin. The sweat evaporates into the air, taking body heat with it.

These methods work well as long as temperature changes are not too great. In extreme cold, the body tries to keep the core temperature at 37°C (98°F) by shivering and breathing harder. But if it drops to about 30°C (86°F), we stop moving and lose consciousness. At about 24°C (76°F), we die. Similarly, if our core temperature rises even a few degrees above normal, we're in danger. The heat of a fever is one way the body fights infection, because heat kills many kinds of germs. But it can kill us, too.

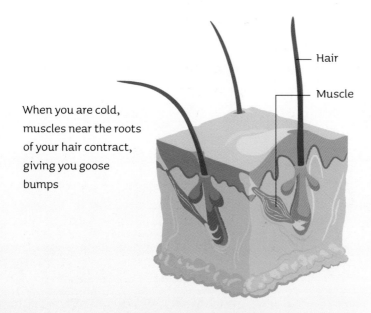

— Hair

— Muscle

When you are cold, muscles near the roots of your hair contract, giving you goose bumps

Old Flames Still Keep Us Warm

Scientists think our earliest human-like ancestors learned how to start a fire over a million years ago. They lived in tropical Africa, where they could get by without fires. But once they had fire, they could move to colder climates all over the world.

Learning to start a fire was a great technical achievement—the first of many to come. And like all technology, it has both good and bad sides. A bonfire can keep us warm and cook our hot dogs. But it can also rage out of control and burn us up.

For thousands of years, people burned animal fat, animal droppings, straw, and wood in their fires. Then, just a few hundred years ago, they started using coal, which they dug out of the ground. Oil and gas were discovered only about 200 years ago. Now the whole world depends on coal, oil, and natural gas for heating, cooking, and running machines, especially cars and trucks. And we are rapidly using up the Earth's supply of these fuels. Scientists estimate that at our present rate of use, all Earth's accessible sources of oil may be gone in 20 to 30 years. And they took about 400 million years to form!

Coal, gas, and oil are called fossil fuels. That's because like fossils, these fuels were formed from the remains of prehistoric plants and animals. Very slowly, over hundreds of millions of years, the bodies of dead plants and animals piled up layer upon layer. They were gradually changed by pressure and by chemical processes. Because the bodies were once living things, they had heat energy from the sun stored in them. And that heat can be recovered when oil, coal, and gas are burned as fuel.

In other words, your family's car runs on sunlight stored in the remains of creatures that lived before the dinosaur age. Coal, oil, and gas are one-time gifts. When they are gone, there won't be any more—at least not for another 400 million years.

Playing with Fire

In nature, plants and animals use and pass on energy to each other in a continuous cycle. For example, the dung beetle lays its eggs in animal droppings, or dung. When the eggs hatch, the dung provides nutrients for the baby beetles. The beetles may then become food for a toad, which may be eaten by a snake. The snake may be eaten by a fox, which will leave dung.

Nature uses energy in a circular pattern, with no waste left over. But people often use energy in a straight line, creating plenty of waste products that pollute the air, water, and soil.

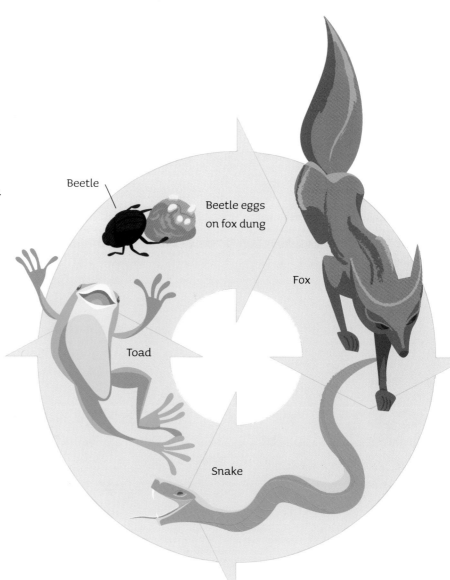

Beetle

Beetle eggs on fox dung

Fox

Toad

Snake

76

Nitrogen and sulfur gases, which pollute the air, land, and water

Oil   Coal   Factories   Cars   Buildings   Waste

Dung beetles will lay their eggs in it, and so the circle begins again. Because one animal's waste is used by another animal, nothing is wasted. The energy keeps getting used and passed on.

Only humans use energy in a way that produces waste. We use energy in a straight line rather than a circle. Using fossil fuels to heat our homes and run our factories and cars creates dangerous waste products that cannot be used but must be disposed of—buried in landfills, dumped into oceans and lakes, or sent into the air.

Waste gases such as nitrogen and sulfur pollute the air we breathe and fall to Earth to damage soil, water, and trees. Fossil fuels also release carbon dioxide, which traps heat. Plants use carbon dioxide in photosynthesis. But we are burning so much fossil fuel today that more carbon dioxide is being released than all the plants in the world can use, and it's building up. Scientists believe this buildup is the major cause of global warming.

It is also foolish to depend on fuels that can't be replaced. Trees will grow again, but coal, oil, and gas will not.

Energy Out the Window

Heat escaping from leaky doors and windows is a common waste of energy. If you combined all the leaky places in a typical home, you would have a hole the size of a basketball!

Save Your Energy

What can we do? For a start, we can stop wasting energy. We can do this in many simple ways, such as turning off lights, TVs, and computers when we aren't using them; recycling and composting our waste; lowering the thermostats in our homes at night, and switching to compact fluorescent light bulbs, which use much less energy than ordinary bulbs. We can choose local, organic foods more often. We can also ride in cars less and walk, skate, or bike instead. It's a lot more fun, and it's good for our health and the Earth's health, too.

We can also make bigger changes as communities and nations. We can pass laws to cut greenhouse gas emissions. We can design "green" homes, schools, and offices that use much less energy. And instead of relying on fossil fuels, we can switch to energy sources that don't pollute and will never run out. For instance, in places near the ocean, the power of tides can drive turbines, which are wheel-like devices with blades that help them rotate. The turbines are connected to generators, which produce electricity. In windy regions, wind can drive turbines to produce electricity. Wind-power technology is growing, making this form of energy increasingly useful. For example, wind power now supplies more than 40 percent of Spain's electricity needs.

And best of all is the bountiful power of sunlight. Perhaps you have a calculator or a game that uses solar power. Solar energy is being used more and more to heat and light buildings, heat water, and generate electricity. For example, a new school in Windsor, Ontario, includes in its many energy-saving features a solar-paneled wall to help supply heat and electricity. In the

future, these and other alternative energy sources may supply a large part of our energy needs.

Like all living things, we share in the Earth's stores of energy. That energy comes from the sun—Earth's fiery star—and burns in every cell of our bodies. Because we need the sun's gifts to live, we must learn to use them wisely, *because we are sunlight.*

How Matt and Muna Use Energy

Matt

Matt lives in Canada. A day in Matt's life might go something like this.

- Matt gets up and switches on radio.
- Goes into bathroom and turns on lights.
- In kitchen, makes toast in toaster and gets juice and milk from fridge.
- Gets on school bus.
- At school, works on computer in fluorescent-lit classroom.
- For lunch, buys chili cooked in school cafeteria.
- After school, gets can of pop from fridge.
- Does homework while watching TV.
- Calls friends on battery-operated cell phone.
- Eats hot dinner with family under hanging light.
- Plays video game.
- Goes to bed and reads comics with flashlight under covers.

Muna

Muna lives in a small village in Nepal. Her day would go more like this.

- Muna gets up and helps her mother make fire in depression in floor of hut (mud floor, thatched roof).
- Carries hay out to oxen in shed.
- Walks to school.
- Does schoolwork by sunlight coming in window; there are no electric lights.
- After school, helps with the work of her family's farm by gathering firewood, carrying big bundle of it on her back.
- At home, eats meal cooked over fire with family; light is candlelight.

People in developed and developing countries leave very different "carbon footprints" on the Earth. On average, each person in developed countries such as Canada uses as much energy in six months as a citizen of developing countries such as Nepal uses in his or her entire lifetime.

The Gift of Prometheus

The early Greeks told this myth about the double-sided nature of fire.

SINCE THE beginning of time, Zeus, the supreme god, had kept fire for the gods' use alone. But one day Prometheus, who was a cunning rogue, stole fire and took it down to men on Earth. (There were no women then.) Zeus was enraged by this bold crime and condemned Prometheus to a gruesome punishment. He was chained to a mountainside for eternity, where every day an eagle came and tore out his liver.

The men were not spared Zeus's fury either. Zeus couldn't take fire away from them, so he gave them something else just as tricky. He created Pandora, the first woman (whose name meant "all gifts") and sent her down to Earth carrying a sealed box, which she was forbidden to open.

Like fire, Pandora was enchantingly beautiful. But she was also uncontrollably curious. One day Pandora opened the box, and out swarmed Zeus's "gifts"—a horde of miseries such as disease, rage, despair, and old age. These miseries would plague humans forever after.

This myth might remind you of the Garden of Eden story. Both tales suggest that as human beings reach out for knowledge and power, they sometimes get more than they bargained for.

Make a Solar Hot-Water Heater

Solar panels are a great way to provide heating and hot water for buildings. Do this activity on a sunny day.

SAFETY TIP: Remember, never look directly at the sun.

WHAT YOU NEED
· Scissors
· A black plastic garbage bag
· 3 large tinfoil cake pans, all the same size
· Masking tape
· A measuring cup
· Plastic wrap
· A thermometer
· A saucer
· A notebook and pen or pencil

WHAT TO DO

1. Start around 10 a.m., when the sun is moving overhead. Cut off a piece of garbage bag big enough to line the inside of one cake pan with a 5-cm (2-inch) overhang. Line the pan, and tape the overhang securely in place against the outside of the pan.

2. Use your measuring cup to fill all 3 pans with the same amount of cold water. Do not overfill the pans. With the thermometer, take the temperature of the water and write it down in your notebook.

3. Fasten plastic wrap securely over the top of the bag-lined pan and one of the other pans. Leave the third pan uncovered.

4. Place the 3 pans outside in a sunny spot. Let them sit for 3 or 4 hours.

5. Check the pans every hour. In your notebook, record the temperature of the water in each pan beside the times you checked.

6. Compare your readings. Does the water heat faster in one pan than in the others? Which pan of water got the hottest? Why do you think it did? Which pan was the solar panel? Was it helpful to have the other pans in the experiment? Why?

WHAT'S GOING ON?
Solar panels in roofs are boxes with a black plate on the bottom and glass or plastic over the top. Black absorbs more heat than other colors. (Isn't a white T-shirt cooler on a hot day than a black one?) The plastic or glass top traps heat inside the box, just as it does on a greenhouse. Air or water can flow through the box in pipes and be carried throughout the house.

83

Magic Candle

Do you know why a candle keeps burning? When you light a candle, the match flame passes heat energy to the candle's wick. The hot wax then combines with oxygen in the air and produces carbon dioxide and water vapor. That's called a chemical reaction. The reaction produces more heat, which keeps the candle burning. You can use this reaction to create a sizzling ending for a magic show.

SAFETY TIP: Have an adult handy when you practice or perform this trick

WHAT YOU NEED:
· A tall, straight-sided candle (not dripless)
· A small knife
· A ruler
· 2 metal skewers or nails
· 2 large equal-sized tin cans or plastic tubs and their tops
· Matches

WHAT TO DO
1. Trim some wax off the bottom of the candle so that the wick sticks out.

2. Measure the length of the candle and find the center. At the center point, push the skewers in, one on each side. Don't push them through to the wick or the candle might break.

3. Balance the skewers on the edges of the cans. The candle should lie straight between the cans. If one end dips, trim it until the candle balances. Place the can tops under the ends of the candle to catch the drips.

4. Light both ends of the candle. Your magic candle will soon begin to seesaw up and down. It will keep on going until the whole candle is burned. Sha-zaam!

WHAT'S GOING ON?
One end of the candle will soon drip more wax than the other. That makes it lighter, so it goes up. The end that goes down drips a big blob, so it becomes lighter and goes back up. And on and on...

Another Idea...

You could use Magic Candle as part of a magic show. Paint the cans or make paper labels. (Trace around the original labels to get the right size.) You might want to draw fiery designs on them such as lightning bolts, suns, or stars. When you are set up, tell your audience that you will use fire power to make a perpetual-motion machine. You could also add Air Magic (page 29) to the show.

5 DEPENDING ON OUR RELATIVES

DID YOU KNOW that you have about six billion creatures living on your body? They especially like to hang out on your forehead, where there is a good supply of oil to shield them from the air. Some prefer to nestle in your eyelashes.

No, we're not talking about lice, ticks, or fleas. We're talking about bacteria and other tiny organisms you'd need a microscope to see. Everybody has them, and you can't get rid of them. Even if you stood in the shower all day, more would land on you from the air seconds after you came out. They like you because you're a great host. You provide them with all kinds of tasty morsels to feed on—skin flakes, oil, dirt, and each other. But don't worry—most of them are harmless. They're just feeding and breeding, living and growing in their habitat. Plants and animals do the same thing in forest, tidepool, prairie, or desert habitats. And we need these bugs.

Your body is a miniature ecosystem. To these bugs, you are part of their environment, just as the town you live in is part of yours.

But Do We Really Need 750,000 Kinds of Insects?

The creatures on your body are not all the same. They include dozens of different species, or kinds, of organisms. Scientists estimate that the Earth is home to about 30 million species of plants and animals. One of them is the species you belong to—the human species, or *Homo sapiens*. In the history of life on Earth, about 30 billion species are thought to have existed. Today, 99.9 percent of these species are now extinct—gone forever, like the dinosaurs.

Earth's present family, though, is truly amazing. Great horned owls, African elephants, monarch butterflies, date palms, killer whales, kangaroos, McIntosh apples—our relatives come in an incredible number of forms. There's a word for that tremendous variety—*biodiversity. Bio* means life, and *diversity* means difference. The idea of biodiversity includes not only beings as different as pigs and pine trees but also many different kinds of pigs and pines. Scientists have discovered about 290,000 species of beetles alone, and they think

Friends Since Forever
Dogs were the first wild animals our ancestors tamed. They have been our companions and friends for at least 15,000 years. It seems cats decided to move in with people about 9,500 years ago.

The Pacific Salmon's Great Circle Game

Salmon alevins are hatched. Later, the young fish, now known as fry, eat small freshwater creatures such as insects, snails, and worms.

Eggs are fertilized.

Bears, birds, and other creatures eat the salmon and then, in their dung, spread nutrients throughout the forest.

Fry also provide food for birds and larger fish.

The bigger the salmon run, the healthier the forest.

When they are 1 month to 3 years old, salmon travel to the ocean.

In the ocean, salmon feed on small ocean creatures. Salmon are food for killer whales, eagles, and seals.

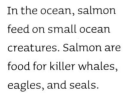

After 2 to 6 years in the ocean, salmon swim back to the stream where they were born and spawn (lay eggs and fertilize them).

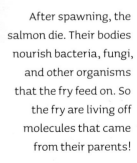

After spawning, the salmon die. Their bodies nourish bacteria, fungi, and other organisms that the fry feed on. So the fry are living off molecules that came from their parents!

that's only a small proportion of the total number that exists. This abundance of species is not an accident or a waste. Like air, water, soil, and energy from the sun, it seems that biodiversity is necessary for life.

All of nature is interconnected. Like the water cycle and the yearly return of the seasons, the lives of all animals and plants are connected in a circular pattern. As one creature is born, it feeds and depends on other creatures, and when it dies, it nourishes and maintains still others.

The salmon cycle is just one example of nature's circular pattern. All 30 million species on Earth today are connected through their life cycles. Everything depends on everything else. Like nuts and bolts in an aircraft, each species is necessary for the health of spaceship Earth.

More Is Better for Ecosystems

Having many species is a great advantage to whole ecosystems when conditions change—say, when the climate becomes drier or a new species arrives. For example, tropical rain forests are crammed with living things. Just a few hectares contain as many species of trees as there are in all of North America. If an insect pest invades a Brazilian rain forest, it meets an army of birds, reptiles, and small mammals that compete with it for space, feed on it, and keep it from spreading beyond a small area. But a temperate rain forest in Washington or British Columbia has far fewer species. When an insect pest such as the spruce budworm invades one of these forests, there aren't so many species to try to stop it. The insect pest can get a foothold and then destroy huge areas of forest.

Scattered over the Earth is a patchwork of ecosystems—coral reefs, tundra, wetlands, prairies, mountains, tropical forests, deserts, temperate forests—and somehow species have found ways to survive in each of these very different habitats. The idea of biodiversity also includes all those ways to survive, or adaptations.

In the Arizona desert, the giant saguaro cactus has a thick, leafless stem that expands when it is filled with water. During the dry season, the stem folds inward in pleats, holding in water. Those features enable it to survive months without rainfall and temperatures that soar to 50°C (120°F).

In a very different environment, deep within the ocean, sea worms swim and breathe, capturing food with feathery, fingerlike projections. They too have learned to live successfully in their home. This variety of adaptations makes it more likely that, no matter what changes take place, some forms of life will survive.

Life Is Everywhere

Life-forms inhabit even the most extreme environments. Geologists have drilled down 4 kilometers (2.5 miles) below the surface of the Earth and found microorganisms in solid rock. A single handful of moss can contain more than 280,000 organisms.

Cultures Have to Be Different, Too

Scientists believe that the modern human species evolved on the Earth somewhere in Africa more than 200,000 years ago. As the population slowly grew, people had to spread out. For most of human history, people were nomadic. They moved from place to place through the seasons, following the growth of plants and animals they needed for food, shelter, and clothing.

Humans gradually moved farther and farther away, exploring different places. Over tens of thousands of years, they traveled thousands of kilometers, mostly on foot and sometimes on rafts and boats, and settled down in such different regions as what we now call Europe, India, and North America. They sailed to Australia and New Zealand and to the islands of the South Pacific. They learned to live in ecosystems as diverse as deserts, mountaintops, seacoasts, grasslands, and rain forests.

People on the grasslands of Europe, Asia, and the Americas learned which wild grasses they could eat and when they would be ripe. They learned to make flour by grinding the seeds of those grasses. On the coast of the Aegean Sea, between present-day Greece and Turkey, people learned how to make hooked harpoons and nets from plant fibers to catch the local fish and shellfish. They found that hollowed-out tree trunks made

A woman from Mali

A Kamayurá from central Brazil

The Earth's many different cultures are the human species' greatest adaptation. Each one has unique abilities and knowledge for survival.

sturdy boats that would take them out to sea. Each group of people passed on its knowledge to the new generation.

As each group learned how to live in its environment, different cultures based on different kinds of food, clothing, and shelter developed. The Incas lived a rugged life high in the cold Andes Mountains in South America. They tamed wild llamas and used them to carry food supplies up and down the steep slopes. They wore warm clothing made from llama wool. In the river valleys of the Middle East, the Sumerians lived very differently. The warm climate and fertile soil gave them plenty to eat, and they could wear light clothing made of woven linen. As cultures spread across the world, groups also developed different languages and beliefs.

This diversity of cultures made humans as a whole better able to adapt to changing conditions. The Sahara Desert was once a grassland with many lakes and rivers. But over thousands of years, the climate became drier and drier, and people gradually moved to other places. They learned how to live in the new areas from the cultures that were already there.

93

Cultural variety gives us a huge pool of talents, skills, and knowledge to draw from. It is the main reason for our success as a species.

Is the Earth Alive?

Have you ever watched an anthill really closely? A famous biologist, Edward O. Wilson, has—and he came up with a whole new way of thinking about them.

Ants are social insects—they cooperate with each other to achieve a goal. The main goal of ants is growth of the colony. To achieve this goal, ants defend their queen to the death, travel many meters to find food supplies, and carry out all the jobs needed to build a strong and secure nest. Some worker ants cut leaves, others dig the nest, and still others look after the baby ants. A large anthill might have a million ants, moving 18,000 kilograms (40,000 pounds) of soil. Long columns of ants reach out from the nest like tentacles, doing their work of finding and gathering food and fighting off predators. If you squint your eyes and let them go out of focus, Wilson says, the busily moving anthill will look like a single animal, with different body parts each doing its job of keeping the whole thing alive.

Another great scientist, James Lovelock, wondered if the Earth might work in the same way. He wondered how the Earth has stayed the same in some important ways over a long period of time. How has the amount of oxygen and carbon dioxide in the air stayed nearly the same for millions of years? Why haven't the oceans boiled away, even though the sun has gotten 25 percent hotter since it was formed? Why haven't the oceans gotten saltier and saltier, since rivers and streams flowing into them are constantly bringing salts dissolved from rock and soil?

His answer was that perhaps the collective action of all living things on Earth have the effect of keeping Earth working properly. If that is true, then just like the parts of your body— eyes and heart and skin—everything on Earth has a role in maintaining the health and life of the whole planet.

The Animal Canoe

*This myth, told by the Ntomba people of
Africa, describes how people and animals
worked together to capture the sun.*

WHEN THE first people were born, in the African country of Zaire, there
was no sunlight, only moonlight. In fact, the people called the moon
"Sun." One day Mokele, the young son of Chief Wai, said to him, "Father,
why does the real sun not shine here?"

"Why, what do you mean?" the chief asked.

"You will see," said Mokele. "I will go and buy the real sun for you!" And he
set about to carve a beautiful canoe from the largest tree in the forest.

When it was finished, the animals of the forest came out to admire it.
First came the wasps, buzzing around Mokele's head. "Let us come with you,"
they whispered in his ear.

"If the owners won't sell you the sun, we will sting them!"

"Good idea!" said Mokele. "Bokendela!" That means "Come on board!"

Just as the wasps were settled into the canoe, the turtle Nkulu crept over.
"I want to come, too," he said.

Mokele laughed. "What can you do? You're too slow!"

"Too slow?" said Nkulu, offended. "I am the first one here of all the wing-
less creatures! Besides, I have magic powers, and I can divine where the sun
is hidden."

"All right—bokendela!" said Mokele.

Next to arrive was the kite bird Nkombe. "I'll help you, too!" he cawed.

"And what can you do?" asked Mokele.

The kite answered, "If the owners won't let you have the sun, I can snatch
it up and fly off with it."

"Fine! Welcome aboard!" said Mokele.

Then came the leopard, the baboon, and the water buffalo. One by one,
all the animals of the forest came to plead their case for going along on

96

the journey. Mokele welcomed them all, and soon the canoe was overflowing with wild creatures.

After many days on the river, the animal canoe finally arrived at the Land of the Sun, which was ruled by the old chief Mokulaka. Mokele greeted him politely and said, "Mokulaka, I'd like to buy the sun from you."

The chief didn't want to give up the sun, but when he saw the canoeful of mighty animals, he knew he would have to be crafty to avoid the sale. "I will gladly let you have it," Mokulaka said, "but wait till my son Yakalaki comes to help us settle on a fair price."

Mokele agreed and sat down to rest. Meanwhile, Mokulaka called his daughter, Molumbu. "Brew up some poison for these strangers," he told her. "I want them all killed!" Molumbu went to carry out her father's order, without noticing that a wasp was hovering nearby. The wasp flew off to Mokele and told him what she had heard. Realizing he could not trust the chief, Mokele decided to steal the sun. He pretended to suspect nothing, and followed Molumbu to her hut.

Now, Mokele was very handsome, and it wasn't long before Molumbu changed her mind about the poison. She threw it on the floor, vowing to elope with Mokele. Meanwhile, the turtle had divined that the sun was hidden in a cave. He set off with the kite, who grasped the sun with his talons and lifted it high in the sky. As the brilliant rays of the sun lit up the Earth for the first time, Mokele and the animals dashed toward their boat. Just then the chief and his son appeared with a pack of warriors and gave chase. But the wasps swooped down, stinging them so fiercely that they fell in defeat.

And so Mokele, his bride, and his animal crew returned home, where the people greeted them with loud cheers and wreaths of flowers. As the animals strolled back to their forest homes, Mokele called out to them. "Thank you, my friends!" he said. "Without the help of each one of you, there would be no sun in the sky today. And now the world is perfect."

Killing Our Kin

At the beginning of this chapter, we said there were about 30 million species on Earth. But that's just one estimate. Other estimates vary from 2 million to 100 million. We really don't know how many there are. Yet some people think we can destroy nature when it suits us and then figure out later how to fix anything that goes wrong.

Suppose you were hired to manage a supermarket. What's the first thing you would do? You would probably find out what was in the store. How many departments are there? What items are sold in each department? What kinds of fruit are there in the produce department? How many kinds of bread are there in the bakery department? What kinds of cheeses, meats, and salads do you have in the deli? Where do you get all these items and what do they cost? You would not be able to run the store unless you knew the answers to these questions.

We have nothing like that kind of information about Earth's life-forms. Biologists have identified a mere 1.5 million species. That means they have seen and put names on that many. It doesn't mean they know how many members of each species there are, what they eat, how they reproduce, or how they interact with other species. Biologists probably know that kind of detail about just a fraction of 1 percent of the species that have been identified. We couldn't manage

99

a supermarket if we had so little information, so how can we think we can manage the world?

It is natural for species to flourish and then die out over time as conditions change. But scientists have identified five periods over the past 500 million years when large numbers of species rapidly became extinct. After each of these periods, or crashes, it took about 10 million years for the Earth to recover to its previous level of biodiversity—but with a very different mix of plants and animals from the mix before the crash. The last of these episodes happened 65 million years ago, when the dinosaurs became extinct. Some people think the dinosaurs were losers because they died off. But remember, they were around for a long time—about 175 million years—while we have been here for a lot less than a million years.

Now we are in a sixth extinction crisis, which is different from all the others. This time, one species alone, *Homo sapiens,* has created it. We are killing species outright or destroying their habitats up to 10,000 times as fast as the normal rate of extinction. Human activities such as clear-cutting forests, damming rivers, polluting the environment, and digging up land to build cities and farms are killing off at least 50,000 species in the world each year—that's six every hour!

Here are a few examples. In British Columbia, more than 142 distinct salmon races have become extinct, and 620 are at high risk of extinction because of damage to stream and river habitats. Biologists believe that only 14 spotted owls are left in all of Canada, because most of their old-growth forest habitat has been logged. And in the world today, one-third of all amphibians, one-quarter of mammals and coniferous trees, and one-eighth of all birds are threatened with extinction.

There are only a few hundred Siberian tigers left in the wild today. Most of this loss is due to intense logging of their forest habitat and to illegal hunting. They are considered critically endangered. Many species today face the same uncertain future.

In North America, more than 6,000 species are estimated to be at risk. But those are just the ones we know about. If scientists have identified only a small fraction of all species, then most are vanishing before they are discovered. A huge number of unknown species disappear forever when their forest, wetland, and coral reef homes are destroyed.

But there are signs of hope. Many people are trying to find ways to stop destroying land and species. Laws have been passed to control pollution from cars and factories. In the United States, free-ranging herds of bison are being returned to parts of Montana and Wyoming. Seed banks have been set up to preserve the seeds of endangered food crops so that they can continue to be grown. Better methods of logging have been developed to allow trees to grow back and prevent the forest ecosystem from being destroyed. But we must do much more. Most important, we humans will have to realize that saving our plant and animal kin means saving ourselves.

We know so little about the Earth's creatures and how they all connect. But like Noah's ark, the Earth sails through the universe carrying its vast cargo of creatures for a reason. We need our relatives—even our own personal colonies of mites and microbes.

Where Are the Bees?

Bees seem to be disappearing in Europe and North America. Their disappearance worries biologists because bees are key pollinators— they carry pollen from one flower to another. Pollinators such as insects, mammals, and birds are essential in nature because most plants, including one-third of our food crops, reproduce by pollination. What can we do? One idea is to plant gardens of native flowering plants to attract native bees. Another is not to use pesticides.

Diary of a Tree

A great way to learn about trees is to "adopt" a special tree for a season or a year.

WHAT YOU NEED
· A notebook and pen or pencil

· Art materials

· A tape measure

· A magnifying glass

· Optional: a camera

WHAT TO DO

1. Pick out a tree. It shouldn't be too far from your home, since you'll be visiting it often. Some things to think about: A deciduous tree (one that sheds its leaves in the fall) will go through more big changes than an evergreen. A large, healthy tree is likely to have a lot happening in it.

2. Find out what kind of tree it is, and then do some research on the Internet or in library books. Write in your notebook anything that interests you about the tree—for example, its scientific name, the types of places where it grows in the world, the climate it prefers, its life cycle, and the animals that depend on it for food or homes.

3. On your first visit, study the tree and write a description of it. Measure the trunk with the tape measure. Look closely at the bark with your magnifying glass and draw a picture of its patterns, or take a rubbing (see "Rub, Press, Print" on the next page). Do you see any animals in the tree? Are nuts or berries forming? Close your eyes. What do you smell? What do you hear?

4. In spring, summer, and fall, take a leaf home. Press it and tape it into your book. If the tree has flowers, you could press one and add it. If you've chosen a fruit tree, make a fruit print for your book (see "Rub, Press, Print").

5. Set aside separate sections in your book for any interesting animals that come to your tree. If birds nest in it, find out what they are and follow what happens over the summer. Be careful not to frighten nesting birds. Move slowly and quietly and don't get too close.

6. Visit your tree once a week for a season or a year, if possible. Each time, write down the date and what you observe. If you have a camera, you could take pictures of the tree in different seasons.

OTHER IDEAS . . .

Give your tree a name. Write a diary entry from the point of view of the tree. If you have a blog, or your class has one, you could post your entries there. Or you could create a blog to write and post photos and drawings about your tree. Ask a parent or your teacher to help you set up the blog.

6 LOVE STORY

MOST ANIMALS TENDERLY care for their babies. When a baby stickleback fish strays from its seaweed nest, the father will pick it up with his mouth and gently return it. Mothers often risk their own lives to protect their babies from harm. Many birds that nest on the ground try to lure intruders away from the nest by putting on an act. The killdeer cries loudly and flops about as if it had a broken wing. The purple sandpiper runs off in a zigzag pattern, its head down and wings drooping to look like back legs, all the while squeaking like a mouse. Some animals, such as the Pacific salmon, even sacrifice their lives for their young. You could say that this is "just" instinct. But this "instinct" shows that love in its many forms is a basic part of life's plan. It may even be necessary for survival.

Love Makes You Healthy

Human beings especially need to love and be loved. Like many other animals, we are born unable to look after ourselves. But we must spend a much longer time than other animals do in the care of adults, growing and learning. And it's not enough just to be fed and clothed and sheltered. In order to thrive, we must also be loved.

Many studies have shown that love in the first years of life is essential for a child to be healthy and happy and able to learn. When a parent loves a child, the child returns that love completely. Love makes us feel secure and teaches us how to love ourselves and others.

Our need to give and receive love is built into our body chemistry. When mothers nurse their babies, the sucking causes a hormone (chemical) to be released in the mother's brain. This hormone starts her milk flowing and at the same time creates strong feelings of love for her baby. Nursing also affects the hormone system of the baby, helping him or her to digest the milk and stimulating the infant's nervous and respiratory systems. The love and bonding that both mother and baby feel help the child survive.

The same bonding hormone (sometimes called the "cuddle chemical") is released when we hug people we love. It works in other animals, too, such as prairie voles. The hormone is released when these small rodents choose mates. As a result, the male becomes very protective, and the pair spends hours grooming each other. Their bond grows so strong that they stay together for life.

The world offers all too many examples of what can happen when young children do not receive love. In Croatia, in Eastern

Europe, wars have separated thousands of children from their families. One group of children, about six years old and just starting school, had many problems. They refused to eat, had nightmares, threw tantrums, and felt sad all the time. Without the love and protection of adults close to them, these children faced an unhappy future.

But when these orphans were adopted by new parents, who gave them the love they needed, many of them changed miraculously. Their sadness disappeared, and they were soon laughing and playing and making friends. Other kids slowly began to feel better but still had some problems. And a few unlucky children didn't get better at all.

This need for love never stops. It seems that just as we need air and water and food, we need to give and receive love, right to the end of our lives.

Relaxed Rats

A study showed that baby rats whose mothers spent the most time licking and grooming them handled stress better when they grew up than other rats did. The mothers' loving touch actually retrained the babies' brains to release fewer stress chemicals.

Even Cells Need Love

Many forms of life are attracted to each other—even cells. All plants and animals are clumps of microscopic cells. You probably have about 45 trillion cells in your body. Cells come in many shapes and sizes, depending on what they do in the body and what kind of body they are in.

Scientists who study cells have discovered that when two cells are brought close together, the thin walls that separate them tend to fuse, and the jelly-like cytoplasm inside the two cells flows together. You could say that cells have a molecular attraction to each other.

Animals are drawn to each other, too. Monkeys, wolves, bees, and many others are social beings that like to live in groups. Animals often clearly show their attraction to each other, by licking, grooming, or nuzzling. When coyotes choose their mates, they celebrate with a long, joyful duet of howling.

Even plants seem to like to be together. Often a houseplant with droopy leaves will perk up when it is placed with other plants.

Different kinds of molecules often bond together to form new substances. Water, for instance, is made up of hydrogen and oxygen atoms bound together. Mutual attraction, or love, is built into life at every level—from animals to plant cells and right down to molecules and atoms. In fact, all matter is attracted to all other matter. It is the way the universe works.

You Need Family, Friends, and Neighbors

What is the best thing about school? Homework? More likely it's being with your friends. We humans, like many other animals, are very social beings. We need love and security, and the place to find them is in families and communities. When we are part of a group of people who share the same beliefs and who value each other, we feel safe. We feel that we belong.

For 99 percent of the time that humans have been on Earth, we lived in small family and tribal groups that moved from place to place. Within these groups, our ancestors learned to hunt and gather food, fought off predators, found mates, formed long-lasting relationships, and shared stories, music, and rituals. The most important consideration in making decisions was the survival and well-being of the group.

Then, about 10,000 years ago, people discovered how to grow their own plants, such as wheat and beans. They also learned how to tame wild animals, such as goats and sheep, and raise them for food. This was the beginning of agriculture. To take care of their crops and animals, people settled down in one place.

Soon farm communities developed, and eventually some of these grew into villages and towns. This was a huge change in a pattern of life that had lasted tens of thousands of years. When people began to live in large towns and cities, they no longer knew all of their neighbors but lived among strangers.

In North America, most people used to live in small communities, but now most live in cities. This change has taken place very rapidly. In big cities, the social "glue" that makes people feel secure and happy is often not there. Even in small towns, people are not as connected to each other as they once were. At the same time, we have all had to get used to more and more technological advances, from airplanes to computers. It is not surprising that many people today feel lonely and cut off from a supporting group.

Today, love in families is a crucial human need. So are strong communities where unemployment is low and there is justice and security. A person who is starving or threatened by war, genocide, or terror will not care about nature. So fighting poverty and hunger, war and terror, is just as important as protecting the environment.

Why Dogs (and Trees) Are Our Best Friends

Do you have a pet? If you do, you know the strong bond we humans can have with other animals. That's love. Or maybe you know the delight of tending a garden and seeing tiny seeds grow into plump red tomatoes, crunchy green beans, or glorious golden sunflowers. That's a kind of love, too.

Those feelings give you a hint of the connection that humans had with the natural world for thousands of years. Through

most of our species' history, the wild creatures around us were companions, not just sources of food. Our first ancestors, who lived in Africa, were surrounded by a huge array of creatures. People listened to the animals' calls at night. They saw and heard the sky come alive with winged creatures, the trees dance in the wind, the plains thunder with hoofbeats. These living beings were not a background to human activity—they were woven into every part of it.

Today there is a growing recognition among scientists that humans thrive in the company of animals. Studies have shown that animals experience many of the same emotions we do, such as joy, sadness, fear, and love. These emotions bind us together. Dogs and cats can be excellent doctors, helping people in hospitals and seniors' homes feel better and sometimes even get better.

Because of our long history of living with other creatures, some scientists believe that humans may have developed a need to be in the company of other beings. Our emotional bond with other living things is another kind of love. Along with air, water, food, and energy, this bond is part of who we are.

Cousins under the Skin, Fur, and Feathers

Recent genetic studies show that 90 percent of our genes are exactly the same as those of the apes. We also have thousands of genes identical to those of cats, dogs, fish, birds, and even trees. In fact, we are related through our genes to every other creature, past and present. First Nations people have always felt this kinship. They recognize it in their clan systems based on animals such as eagles and ravens.

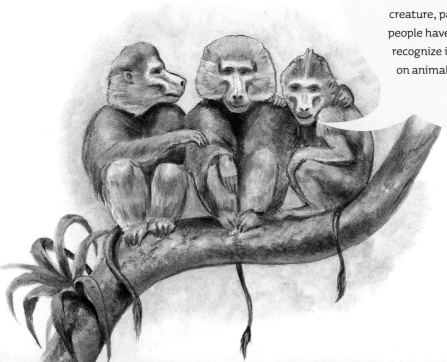

Diary of a Hunter-Gatherer

Imagine that you are a child growing up long, long ago. Use the Internet or books to research an ancient culture that interests you. Maybe you belong to a very early group of nomads, who hunt wild animals and pick grasses and berries for food. Or you might be part of a later culture, such as the Incas, Celts, or Vikings. Write a diary entry describing a day or a week in your life. Describe your home, clothes, food, and daily activities. Perhaps record a conversation. You could also add drawings to illustrate your diary. Or you could do the whole activity in pictures, as a comic strip or graphic story.

7 BEYOND AWESOME

WHERE DID WE come from? Why are we here? What happens to us after we die?

Have you ever asked yourself those questions? If so, you're like most of the people who have ever lived on Earth. From the earliest times, people have tried to answer these questions through stories and myths.

There are thousands of these stories. According to different versions, humans were shaped out of clay and water, carved from twigs, or hatched from a huge egg. Most of these creation myths start with the same idea—humans were made from the Earth's elements, just as science says we were.

Creation Stories

Creation myths were considered the most sacred of all stories. They gave shape to and made sense of the world people lived in. They gave them rules to live by. And they gave them reasons for the cruelties and misfortunes of life. Humans had qualities that other animals did not, such as greed, pride, and ambition. People knew these qualities caused much of the pain in the world and wanted explanations for them.

Most of our stories tell about a time when humans disobeyed their gods, tried to be gods themselves, and were punished for it. In the Prometheus myth, Pandora opens the forbidden box and lets loose a rain of evils on the world. In the story of the Garden of Eden, Adam and Eve eat the apple from the tree of knowledge and for their disobedience are banished from the garden.

Blame It on the Brain

Humans are highly curious animals with a drive to learn more and more about their world. This curiosity comes from our brain. We humans have a very large and complex brain. It has given us not only curiosity but also consciousness, memory, and the ability to plan ahead. We can learn from experience, and unlike other animals, we can pass on our knowledge to the next generation. For this reason, we have evolved much faster than ordinary evolution would have allowed.

It's All in Your Head

Our brain gives us consciousness, memory, and the ability to plan ahead. This brain map shows areas of the brain that control different body functions.

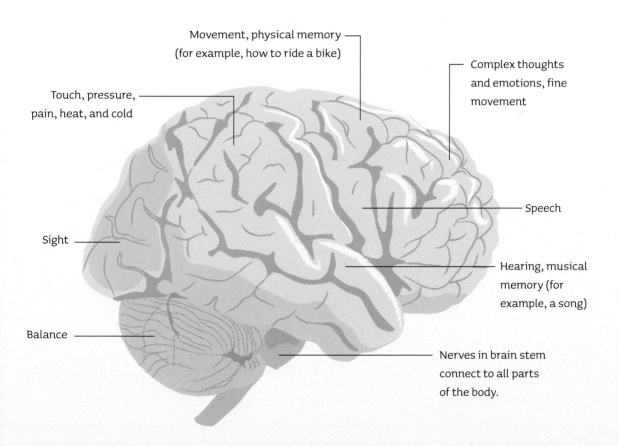

Movement, physical memory (for example, how to ride a bike)

Complex thoughts and emotions, fine movement

Touch, pressure, pain, heat, and cold

Speech

Sight

Hearing, musical memory (for example, a song)

Balance

Nerves in brain stem connect to all parts of the body.

Memories are stored in different parts of the brain.

119

But consciousness has also given us the sorrowful knowledge that we will die. We need our stories to help us accept this greatest mystery of all. All cultures have believed in a power greater than human power, in some kind of life after death, and in something within us that is eternal—our soul or spirit.

"We have to feel the heartbeats of the trees, because trees are living beings like us."

SUNDERLAL BAHUGUNA, SPOKESPERSON
FOR THE CHIPKO MOVEMENT

The Gifts of Spider Woman

Here is a creation story told by the Hopi people.

THE HOPI people believed that the great god of the universe, Sotuknang, commanded his helper-goddess, Spider Woman, to create the first people. When she had done this, she took a long look at her handiwork. She decided some finishing touches were needed. She said to Sotuknang: "As you have commanded me, I have created these First People. They are fully and firmly formed; they are properly colored; they have life; they have movement. But they cannot talk. That is the proper thing they lack. So I want you to give them speech. Also the wisdom and power to reproduce, so that they may enjoy their life, and give thanks to the Creator."

Inspiration

The word "inspiration"—which can mean either a breath or a brilliant idea—and the word "spirit" are both related to the Latin word *spirare,* meaning "breathe." Spirit, the soul, creation, breath, and life have long been connected in human thought.

Picturing the World

Traditional cultures today, like our earliest ancestors, see the world in a very different way from modern cultures. To people in traditional cultures—such as the Aborigines in Australia, the Yanomami people in Brazil, or the Haida people on the west coast of Canada—everything is alive with spirit. The mountains, forests, rivers, winds, and lakes are ruled by gods. Each tree, stone, or animal may have a soul like ours. And the spirits of the dead and yet-to-be-born may be present around us. People are just one part of this grand symphony of souls. One of our responsibilities in keeping the universe working as it should is to carry out various rituals and sacred ceremonies.

The Aborigines in Australia, for instance, tell a beautiful story about how the world began. They say the Ancestors sang it into existence. The people's role is to keep the Earth sacred by continuing to sing the ancient songs, which have been handed down through the generations. They believe that their land is sacred and that each part of it has a spirit. Sometimes one of the spirits will decide to take on human form for a while, and that's how people are born. Each person, then, is truly joined with a particular part of the Earth and will suffer and die if he or she wanders too far from home.

This feeling of being part of a spirit-filled world is not the way most modern people feel today. Instead, many of us see ourselves as separate from our environment. You are you, and the rest of the world is outside you. When you look at a tree, you know it isn't a part of you, right? And it certainly doesn't have a soul. We take that idea of reality for granted, without even thinking about it.

At some point in history, we lost our feeling of spiritual connection to the rest of the world. We stopped seeing a spirit in the tree and began taking the tree's measurements. (Let's see, it's so many meters high, its leaves are shaped in such-and-such a way, and we can get so much money for it if we cut it down.) The tree was no longer our kin but something completely different from us. As we lost that connection, we also began to make bigger and bigger changes to our world.

And so we have created our own universe, filled with office buildings and cars and sports stadiums and shopping malls and all the other things that in a city can seem much more real and important than rivers and birds. Our human-made world doesn't have spirits in it—it has things. But this is a lonely way to live. Separated from the spirits of the Earth, we are strangers in our own home.

Some Things Are Sacred

Think about your room at home. Has anyone ever said to you, "This room is a mess! You don't need all that junk"? But to you, it's probably a great room, and you don't want to part with a thing. You'd never give up your catcher's mitt, a present from your dad. And you certainly need your books—you can remember reading every one, or having them read to you, for the first time. Last year's Halloween space-monster costume has to stay. It's so cool, and besides you made it yourself. How about that beat-up old teddy you had when you were small? Or those seashells you got five summers ago at your grandma's? Nope. Everything in your room is part of what makes it special to you. Even the really old things are important, because they bring back memories you want to keep in your mind and heart.

Not everybody would think that the things in your room are valuable, but they mean a lot to you. They have a kind of spiritual value. Spiritual values have to do with feelings and memories. They have nothing to do with money. They are priceless.

Aboriginal people believe that nature has deep spiritual value. Many other people, including scientists, agree. When you walk through a pine-scented forest or along the shores of a sparkling lake, you feel refreshed and connected to the Earth. It is a sacred place.

An American psychoanalyst and author named Robert Jay Lifton once told an amazing story about what happened after the bombing of Hiroshima, a city in Japan, at the end of World War II. The atomic bomb had destroyed the city and killed about 100,000 people. The blast had also sent a cloud of deadly atomic rays across the city, causing a terrible sickness.

Afterward, a rumor spread that nothing would ever grow on that ground again. And this possibility was a greater horror to the people than all the death and destruction caused by the bomb itself. Only after grass began to grow again did they start to feel better.

People need to know that nature will continue. Without thinking about it, we count on the sounds of birds and crickets, the ebb and flow of the tides, the blossoming of trees every spring. It could be that spiritual connection to creation is another of our absolute needs, just like earth, water, air, fire, our plant and animal kin, and love.

126

Myth Making

Create your own myth in words or pictures. Think about the stories in this book and what they have in common. Your myth might be about how the world began. Or it might be about where one part of the world—bees or snakes or the wind—came from. You'll probably want to include some interesting animals, people, or both who have a problem to solve. You could add a few strange details or surprising events.

127

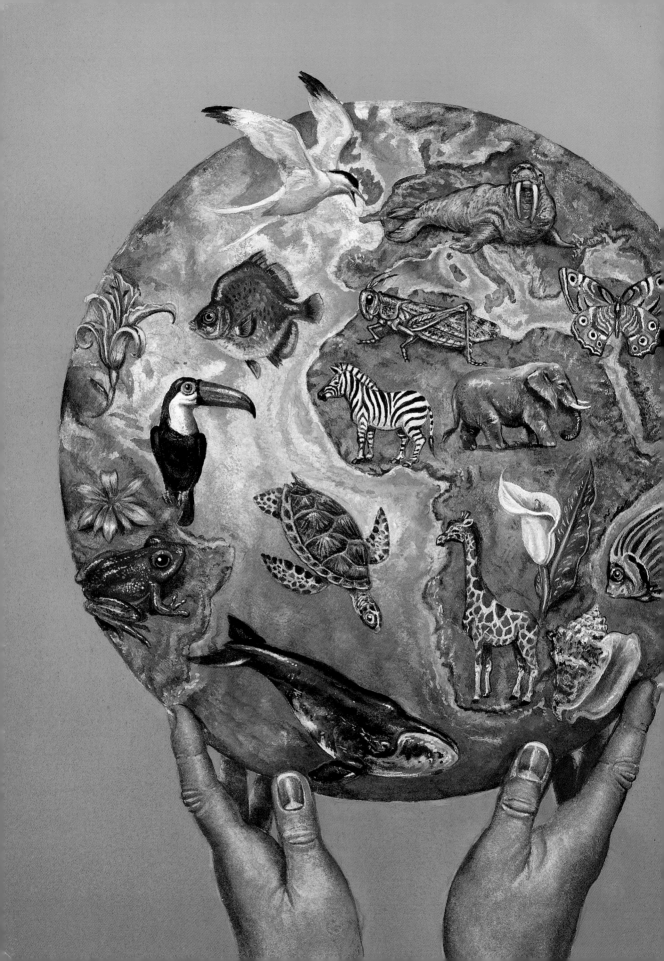

8 IT'S YOUR WORLD NOW

YOU WILL SPEND most of your life in the 21st century. This is your world, and it's a wonderful world—but it has some problems. Global warming, pollution, habitat destruction, species extinction, devastation of the sea and its creatures, energy shortages—these are big challenges that require big efforts from nations working together. But smaller actions by individuals and groups—if there are enough of them—can be very powerful, too. Each one of us can do something to help.

"But I'm just a kid—I can't save the world."

Young people often know more about what's happening to the environment than adults do. And many of them are working hard to change things. The following stories are just a few examples of what kids and teenagers can do.

Cooling Coventry

In 2006, nine-year-old Colin Carlson, of Coventry, Connecticut, was invited to go on a special National Geographic *kids' expedition to the Galápagos Islands. He didn't know he would find something there even more surprising than giant turtles.*

THE BIG thing I saw in the Galápagos—or didn't see, really—was penguins. I was expecting to see a lot of Galápagos penguins, and we only saw five during the whole trip. That's because global warming (and the increase in severe storms that global warming is causing) is greatly reducing the penguin population. This really got me thinking about climate change. I was concerned that the estimated rise in sea levels over the next 40 years could entirely destroy the Islands' precious ecosystem. When I got back home, I took a conservation biology class and saw Al Gore's film, *An Inconvenient Truth*. That was the final motivation I needed to start working to fight global warming.

I started the Cool Coventry Club that fall, after I turned 10. Over the next two years I organized dozens of events in towns and schools in the area, gave speeches, handed out leaflets, and ran petition drives. I talked to business and government leaders and set up a web site to spread the message further. The web site invites people to "join the club" by pledging to make three changes to lower their

energy use. I also set up the Keep Us Cool Initiative, a Listserv where students can share ideas across the country or anywhere in the world.

At first, lots of people didn't believe me when I talked about global warming or didn't understand how it affected *them*. So I've tried to stress messages such as saving money by saving energy, since those are things people tend to agree on. I think my town has gotten a lot more energy conscious since I've been working on this issue. The library has changed to compact fluorescent lighting, the town council has committed to purchasing clean energy, and enough people signed up for our state residential clean-energy option to earn a free solar panel system for the town. It really makes me feel good when people stop me on the street to tell me what they are doing to reduce their carbon footprint.

What I would like to say to young people is, have faith in yourself and your ability to make a difference, and don't listen if people tell you that you can't. Even a small difference creates a ripple effect over time, and you'll be amazed when you look back and see how much you have accomplished, both directly and indirectly. Our climate needs help today, so don't wait to get started. You can work on your own or with friends or family. Any way you choose to spread the word will help the planet.

It's in the Bag

Millions of plastic grocery bags are used once, get tossed in the garbage, and end up in a landfill—what a waste! In 2007, the Make a Difference Club at Bench Elementary School in Cowichan Bay, British Columbia, decided to tackle the problem in their community. First, club members took a survey of how students used plastic bags and showed an educational video.

EcoTeam Works for Greener Schools

Alison Lee was a grade 10 student at Marc Garneau C.I. in Toronto, Ontario, when she started the EcoTeam club to raise environmental awareness at her school. By the second year, the club's work had spread out to the entire city.

IN OUR first year, we had only 10 members in a school of 2,000. We started by taking a survey of students' carbon footprints—how much energy they were using. We then made sure each class had a recycling bin, and trays to stack paper for re-use. To reduce litter and promote school pride, we painted colorful designs on the hallway garbage bins.

The next year we had 30 members, and we added a "Lights Off" monitoring program to make sure lights were turned off when not in use. We also hosted an open house for secondary school groups interested in starting an environmental team. We gave them a lot of advice about student leadership, which is what our club relies on. And we put on a "Green Screens" film festival of short environmental films created by students. The films emphasized action on environmental issues and lent ideas to those just starting out.

Another project we started was an annual student cleanup of Toronto

Then they launched a campaign of skits, movies, and presentations about plastic bags. They also sold reusable cloth bags and donated the money they made to charities. The students started with local schools and the city council and branched out to regional politicians and other towns in the area. At the end of the year, they found that the use of plastic bags had dropped in the city as a whole and that student use was down 68 percent.

parks. We met regularly with students from five other schools to plan it out. There were four cleanup events around the city for Earth Week 2008. The cleanup by my EcoTeam took place at Sunnybrook Park and attracted students from three other schools. There was television and newspaper coverage at a few of the cleanups, as well as food and beverage donations from local stores. Local schools working together to improve our community was a great example of city-wide teamwork!

This year, our third year, we have 50 members. I have encouraged many smaller groups to form and take on more projects, and in this way, our impact has broadened. I am also part of a city environmental council called STEP (Students of Toronto for Environmental Progress). We work with the people who provide schools with resources, such as purchasing products and nutritional services. We hope to encourage schools to adopt more sustainable practices, such as buying only 100-percent recycled copy paper. Changes like that increasingly reflect what students want.

The Idle-Free Girls

Katelyn Morran, Rachel Perrella, Neely Swanson, and Destiny Gulewich are grade 7 students at Stonewall Centennial School in Stonewall, Manitoba. The girls have spread their idle-free message throughout their town and in Winnipeg and the surrounding area.

IT ALL started when we studied weather and climate change in grade 5 and we became concerned about global warming. The four of us wanted to make a difference. We decided to choose a project that could have a big impact on the environment, so we started an anti-idling campaign.

Our goal was to make our community idle free, where people would not idle their vehicles for more than 10 seconds. We wanted to educate youth and adults about the harmful effects of leaving a car's motor running when you are not driving it. Idling not only adds to global warming but wastes fuel and pollutes the air, and pollution can cause asthma and other health problems. We created student and public awareness through presentations, media events, the Internet, displays, pamphlets, and Idle-Free Zone signs. Soon after making our presentations to the town council, Idle-Free signs were put up all around town, and we became known as the Idle-Free Girls. The support for our campaign has been incredible. People are always telling us they notice there is a lot less idling in town now.

School Today—Yum!

The lucky kids at James Thompson Elementary School in Richmond, British Columbia, know where food comes from—their own garden. Their school takes part in the Terra Nova Schoolyard Garden Project, run by Vancouver chef Ian Lai. Students come to the garden to plant seeds, nurture plants, harvest their crops, and finally cook and eat the food they have grown. Worm composting bins help reduce waste. In an adjoining classroom and kitchen, students learn about good nutrition, organic gardening, and caring for the land. And the garden saves energy because the food does not have to be trucked long distances.

What do the students say about their garden?

"Since I have been coming to the garden I have been thinking a lot more about what I put in my stomach."
MALYKH LOPEZ, *age 10*

"We learned about the diversity of life and how it works."
PATRICK RUVALCABA, *age 10*

"I learned that fruits and vegetables are healthier for you than the food I usually eat."
PATRISSE CHAN, *age 10*

"Last year we harvested oats. Then we dried the oats and made bread with them. It tasted good. It is very exciting growing food!"
KLARA MARSH, *age 8*

135

First, Clean Up the Backyard

So, you want to make a difference, but how do you get started? Here are some simple things you can do for the Earth—and yourself.

- Find out how ordinary things work—such as sewage, garbage, water, electricity, food, clothing. Where do they start? What happens to them? Where do they go?

- At home and at school, practice the three *R*'s: Reduce, Reuse, Recycle—especially Reduce. That means buying and using less.

- Ask yourself before buying something: Do I really need this?

- Walk, bike, or Rollerblade as much as possible, rather than asking someone to drive you.

- Take an inventory of your home (see "Grade Your Home for Greenness," page 143) to see if there are ways your family could save energy.

- Make compost from vegetable and fruit leftovers.

- Switch from regular light bulbs to compact fluorescent bulbs. They use much less energy and last much longer.

- Plant trees.

- Take waste-free lunches to school packed in reusable containers.

- Plant an organic garden. Use natural fertilizers, not chemicals, on your lawn, too.

- Check out environmental groups in your area and volunteer. These groups need help with all kinds of projects, such as planting trees, clearing garbage off a beach, or pulling weeds that are destroying a wetland habitat.

- Start an environmental club at your school.

- Some school classes produce podcasts—online radio programs. If yours does, use it to spread the word about the environment— maybe include a Green Tip of the Day. If you don't have a podcast, ask your teacher about setting one up.

- Get out into nature whenever you can. And when you get there— let it amaze you!

The Cost of Stuff

Many natural resources, such as oil, trees, and aluminum, are used to make, advertise, and sell all the things we buy. Then there is the waste that these purchases create—the bags and boxes they come in, the advertising flyers, and the things themselves when we throw them away. This mountain of garbage gets burned in incinerators, dumped into lakes, or buried in the ground, where it can contaminate the air, water, and soil.

Lifting Up the Sky

The Snohomish people tell this story.

WHEN THE Creator made the world, he started in the east. Then he moved slowly westward. In a big sack, he carried many languages, and as he went along creating tribes of people here and there, he gave each one a language. When he came to Puget Sound, in the state of Washington, he liked it so much he decided to stop there. But he still had a lot of languages in his sack, so he scattered them all around the area.

Because they spoke so many different languages, the people couldn't talk to each other. But it turned out that all of them agreed on one thing—the Creator had made the sky much too low. Tall people were always bumping their heads on it. And sometimes people would do something they were forbidden to do. They would climb up into the tall trees and enter the Sky World.

Finally, the wisest elders of all the tribes had a meeting to see what could be done about the sky. They decided they would have to try to push it up. But how could they do that?

"We can do it if we get together and push at the same time," said one elder. "We will need all the people and the animals and the birds."

"But how will we know when to push?" said another elder. "We speak so many different languages. How can we get everyone to push together?"

The elders thought about this for a while. Finally, one of the elders said, "Why don't we use a signal? When we have everything ready and it is time to push, one of us can shout 'Ya-hoh!' That means 'Lift together' in all our languages." And so it was agreed.

The wise men went back to their villages and spread the word about the sky-lifting attempt. They told the people and the animals and the birds where and on what day the event would take place and what the signal would be to push together. Then everyone got busy making poles from the tallest pine trees, to be used in pushing against the sky.

When the big day came, everyone gathered at the chosen spot. The people and animals lifted their poles till they touched the sky. Then, when the wise men shouted "Ya-hoh!" they all pushed as hard as they could. The sky moved a couple of centimeters (an inch). On the second "Ya-hoh!" everyone pushed again, and the sky moved up just a bit more. Again the signal was given, and again the assembled group pushed with all its might.

All day the signal rang out, and each time the people pushed until their muscles ached and the sweat ran down their bodies. At last, they gave one final mighty heave, and the sky moved up to where it is now. Since then, people and animals have walked around freely without bumping their heads against the sky, and no one has been able to enter the Sky World. And the Snohomish people still say, "Ya-hoh!" when they are doing hard work or lifting something heavy, such as a canoe. When they hear this signal, they use every bit of their strength to accomplish the task together.

139

Saving a Rain Forest

The people of Saltspring Island in British Columbia didn't stage a protest to save their ecologically valuable Creekside Rainforest from being logged and developed. They simply raised $1 million and bought it from the developers. With the help of the Land Conservancy of B.C., they raised the money every way they could think of. They staged a play and put on an art exhibit, and kids sold homemade cards and birdhouses.

Trust in Nature

Nature has a remarkable ability to heal itself, given half a chance. Fish returned to the River Thames in England after anti-pollution laws were passed, and plants started growing again around Sudbury, Ontario, after metal-making factories installed scrubbers, which cut down on the toxic gases going into the air.

Many people are working today to bring about bigger miracles. But we humans must be creative and generous and strong enough to make that happen. Some people say that protecting the environment costs too much. They say there are more important things than grizzly bears and prairies and rivers. But what can be more important than this precious home we share?

The Earth has sailed through the universe for billions of years, slowly creating the perfect conditions for life in all its fabulous variety. We don't know how that works. We can't control the tides or the seasons. We can't create a tropical forest and fill it with hundreds of thousands of species all working together to keep it healthy. Only nature can do these things. All we can do is try to let nature keep on doing them.

Our survival depends on remembering who we are. We are the Earth—part of the air, water, soil, and energy of the world; surrounded by our kin, the plants and animals that keep the world livable for us; beings with love in our hearts and life in our souls. It is up to us to protect those things so that they will be around for many generations to come.

Paint the Town White

Since white surfaces reflect more sunlight back to space than dark surfaces do, we could fight global warming simply by painting roofs white. In fact, scientists estimate that making the roofs and pavements white in all cities in hot and temperate climates would cut 44 billion tonnes of greenhouse gas emissions per year. That is more than the whole world pumps out. California already requires that all flat roofs in the state be white and new sloped roofs be light-colored.

Grade Your Home
for Greenness

*We can help the environment a lot
right in our own homes. So how are you
doing? Take a tour and answer this
"green home" quiz.*

1. If possible, do you recycle
   rather than throw these away?
   1 point each

A. Cans_____

B. Paper and cardboard_____

C. Glass bottles_____

D. Plastic bottles_____

E. Clothes you don't wear anymore_____

2. Do you make compost out of

A. kitchen waste?

B. yard waste?

   5 points each _____

3. Do you reuse old containers
   (plastic tubs, cans, boxes, jars, and
   so on) for other things? List uses:
   2 points each, up to 10 points, or 5 uses

   _____

   _____

   _____

   _____

   _____

   _____

   _____

4. Do you take dangerous garbage
   to a hazardous waste depot?
   10 points _____

   Add a bonus point if you can pick
   out the only one of the following
   items that is *not* hazardous:

   batteries, paint, turpentine, car
   battery acid, drain cleaner, medicines,
   vinegar, lighter fluid, pesticides,
   needles, aerosol spray cans

   _____

5. Do you use compact
   fluorescent light bulbs?
   5 points for all, 2 points for some _____

6. Do you turn out lights
   when leaving a room?
   5 points _____

7. In winter, do you keep the house
   temperature coolish during the
   day (you can wear a sweater)
   and even cooler at night?
   10 points _____

8. In summer, do you water lawns
   not more than once or twice a week?
   10 points _____

9. Do you use safer, homemade alternatives or buy "green" products for the following?
1 point each

A. Window cleaner_____

B. Laundry detergent _____

C. Pesticides and weed killers_____

D. Floor cleaners _____

E. Anything else? _____

10. Does your family have an alternative-energy system (solar, wind, geothermal) for anything?
10 points _____

11. Add any green product or habit your family has that is not listed above. (For example, an energy-saving appliance such as a fridge or stove—it might have an "Energy Star" label; walking, biking, or taking public transportation instead of traveling by car; choosing products with the least packaging or the most environmentally friendly packaging.)
5 points each up to 20 points, or 4 examples _____
_____
_____
_____

12. Now subtract 1 point for every leaky tap you find.
Minus _____

13. Count how many electric appliances you have in the house. You might get a shock! Count any light bulb and don't forget small items such as electric toothbrushes and can openers. Discuss with your family whether you are using any appliances you could do without.
Subtract 1 point for each unnecessary appliance _____

Add (and subtract) the points to get your home's Green Grade:

_____ 80 to 100
Bright green like a summer leaf

_____ 60 to 79
Yellow-green like a spring leaf

_____ 40 to 59
Pale yellow and ready to fall

_____ Under 40
You're on the ground!

144

ABORIGINAL Having to do with peoples who have inhabited a land since the earliest times—for example, Native Canadians and Americans and Australian Aborigines.

ADAPTATION A change in an organism or species that helps it survive in a new environment.

AIR SACS Tiny balloon-like pouches in the lungs that let oxygen pass into the blood vessels and let carbon dioxide pass out.

ARGON One of the less plentiful gases in the Earth's atmosphere, making up only about 1 percent of it.

ATMOSPHERE The layer of gases surrounding the Earth.

ATOM The smallest particle of matter.

BIODIVERSITY The variety of plants, animals, and ecosystems in the world.

BRONCHI Tubes in the lungs that branch out like tree branches from the windpipe. Singular is *bronchus*.

BRONCHIOLES Smaller tubes that branch out from the bronchi.

CARBOHYDRATES A group of substances in food that supply energy. Some foods that are good sources of carbohydrates are vegetables, fruit, and bread.

CARBON DIOXIDE A gas that animals breathe out into the air and that plants take in from the air.

CARBON FOOTPRINT The amount of carbon dioxide released by human activities such as driving cars, heating our homes, buying things made in factories, eating food transported long distances by plane or truck, and so on.

CELL The basic unit of life. Each cell is enclosed by a membrane that separates it from other cells and the environment.

COAL A hard black rock that formed over millions of years from plant remains. Coal is used as a fuel.

CONDENSATION The changing of a gas into a liquid. For example, water vapor (a gas) condenses in clouds and may fall as rain (a liquid).

DEVELOPED COUNTRY A country that is relatively rich, with many industries and technological advances—for example, Canada, the United States, Australia, and Japan.

145

DEVELOPING COUNTRY A country that is beginning to have more industries and technological advances but is still relatively poor—for example, Kenya, Guatemala, and Thailand.

ECOSYSTEM A community of interacting animals and plants and their environment.

ENERGY The ability to do work. Energy is never created or lost but only changed from one form to another.

ESOPHAGUS A tube through which food passes from the mouth to the stomach.

EVAPORATION The changing of a liquid into a gas. For example, water (a liquid) changes into water vapor (a gas) when you boil it.

EVOLVE To develop gradually.

EXTINCT SPECIES A species of animal or plant that no longer exists in the world; all members of the species have died. The dinosaur *Tyrannosaurus rex* is an example of an extinct species.

FOSSIL FUEL Coal, oil, or gas, which formed in the Earth billions of years ago from the remains of animals and plants and which we burn for energy.

FUNGI A group of organisms that are similar to plants but do not have chlorophyll and reproduce by means of spores rather than seeds. Mushrooms, yeast, and mold are examples of fungi. Singular is *fungus*.

GAS A usually invisible substance that does not have shape or volume. Water vapor (steam) is an example of a gas.

GENES The material in cells that is passed on from generation to generation. These "blueprints" of life tell cells how to carry out the bodily processes that make life possible. Genes also determine features such as what color your eyes and hair are, how tall you are, and whether you are right- or left-handed.

GRAVITY The force that pulls objects toward the Earth. For example, if you drop a pencil, gravity will make it fall to the floor rather than float in the air or fly up.

GREENHOUSE GAS A gas that traps heat from the sun and holds it in the atmosphere. The main greenhouse gases are carbon dioxide, water vapor, methane, and nitrous oxide.

HABITAT A natural area where particular plants or animals live. A river, for example, might be the habitat of several species of fish, insects, mammals, and plants.

HYDROGEN The lightest gas in the atmosphere. Water molecules are made up of hydrogen and oxygen atoms.

METABOLISM The sum of the chemical processes in an organism that provide energy and growth.

MICROORGANISM A plant or animal that is so small it can only be seen by looking through a microscope.

MICROSCOPIC Very small; can only be seen by looking through a microscope.

MINERAL A natural material that is not formed from animals or plants. Salt, stone, and iron are examples of minerals.

MOLECULE A group of atoms. For example, the water molecule is made up of two hydrogen atoms and one oxygen atom.

MYTH A traditional story, usually about gods, ancestors, or heroes, that explains the beliefs and values of a culture.

NATURAL GAS Gas that formed over millions of years from the remains of plants and animals and was trapped beneath the Earth's crust. Natural gas is used as a fuel.

NUTRIENT A substance in food that is necessary for life. Fats, carbohydrates, proteins, vitamins, and minerals are examples of nutrients.

OIL A thick liquid that formed over millions of years from the remains of plants and animals and was trapped beneath the Earth's crust. Oil is used mainly as a fuel.

OLFACTORY BULB A small patch of cells high up inside the nose that picks up smells in the air we breathe in and sends messages about them to the brain.

ORGANIC Coming from plants or animals.

ORGANISM A living plant or animal.

OXYGEN An element in the air that all animals and plants need to live because it is the fuel we burn to release energy.

OZONE LAYER A thin layer in the atmosphere surrounding the Earth that shields us from most of the sun's ultraviolet light rays.

PHOTOSYNTHESIS The process by which green plants take in carbon dioxide and water and, using sunlight, make food and release oxygen.

PITUITARY GLAND A small gland at the bottom of the brain that releases substances that are essential for growth and various body processes.

POLLINATOR Something that carries pollen from one flowering plant to another. Examples are bees, butterflies, birds, mammals, and the wind.

POLLUTANT A substance that doesn't normally belong somewhere and upsets the surroundings.

PROTEINS A group of substances in food that are needed for health and life. Some foods that are good sources of proteins are meat, eggs, and nuts.

RADIATION The sending out of waves of heat or light.

SPECIES A group of plants or animals that share certain characteristics and can reproduce with each other. The horse and the human being are examples of species.

TRADITIONAL CULTURE A group of people whose shared values, beliefs, and practices have been handed down from generation to generation.

TROPOSPHERE The lowest layer of the atmosphere, in which living things exist and weather takes place.

ULTRAVIOLET LIGHT Light rays from the sun that can be harmful to living things.

WATER CYCLE The constant circulation of water through the Earth and living things. Water vapor condenses in clouds and falls to Earth as rain or snow; collects in soil, water, and organisms; and is released back into the air through breath, sweat, and evaporation.

WEATHERING The breaking down of rocks and other materials by forces such as wind, rain, and ice.

Questions

1. What essential gas takes up about 21 percent of our atmosphere?

2. We breathe in carbon dioxide and breathe out oxygen. *True or false?*

3. Plants take in carbon dioxide and release oxygen into the air in a process called _____.

4. How does the oxygen you breathe into your lungs reach your bloodstream?

5. The layer of air in which we live and where weather happens is the _____.

6. What do most scientists believe is the main cause of global warming?

7. What is the ozone layer, and why do we need it?

8. Greenhouse gases are bad for the atmosphere. *True or false?*

9. Where is most of your body's water located?

10. How much water do you need each day?

11. You need water because *(check all the right answers)*:

   A. It tastes good.

   B. It contains carbohydrates.

   C. It cures warts and other skin diseases.

   D. It helps your heart keep pumping.

12. A molecule of sweat off your body might turn up later in *(check all the right answers)*:

   A. A tree

   B. A cloud

   C. Someone else's body

   D. The ocean

13. The Earth's water cycle changes salty water into _____.

14. Which of the following are good ways to use less water during the day? *(Check all the right answers.)*

   A. When you are brushing your teeth, turn the tap on and off instead of letting it run the whole time.

   B. Drink less water.

   C. Have a quick shower rather than a bath, especially if your shower has a water-saving showerhead.

   D. If you notice a tap leaking at home or school, report it to an adult in charge of fixing it.

15. All your food comes from the soil.
    True or *false?*

16. What are the main nutrients in food
    that you need to be healthy?

17. Wind, rain, and ice break down rocks
    into small bits in a process called
    _____ .

18. What organisms might
    you find in the soil?

19. How do plants and
    animals enrich the soil?

20. How can farmers
    make the soil healthier?
    (*Check all the right answers.*)

    A. Use chemical fertilizers.

    B. Use powerful chemical pesticides to
       kill every bug and weed.

    C. Plant a variety of crops.

    D. Right after harvesting one crop,
       plant another one.

21. Most people in the world eat mainly
    _____ .

22. Where does all the energy that
    makes life possible come from?

23. What part of your body stays
    the same temperature all the time?

24. What did our early ancestors learn to
    do that allowed them to travel all over
    the world, even to cold regions?

25. Why are coal, oil, and gas
    called fossil fuels?

26. What are the three main ways your
    body keeps your inner core warm?

27. What are three ways you could use
    less energy during the day?

28. You provide a _____ for
    about six billion microscopic
    creatures.

29. The Earth has 10 to 15 million
    _____ of plants and animals.

30. How do salmon help the trees
    in the forest?

31. We should try to protect the many
    different species of plants and animals
    in the world (biodiversity) because
    (*check all the right answers*):

    A. All species are connected through
       their cycles.

    B. Biodiversity helps species survive
       when conditions change.

    C. Biodiversity makes our lives more
       beautiful and interesting.

32. Why is it important to protect whole
    ecosystems and not just individual
    plant and animal species?

33. What is an extinction crisis?

34. What is causing our present
    extinction crisis?

35. What happens when two cells
    are brought close together?

36. What are social animals?

37. Besides food and shelter, what do
    babies need to grow and be healthy?

38. Humans have completely
    different genes from other animals.
    True or false?

39. Why have people throughout
    history told creation stories?

40. What do we humans have that makes
    us most different from other animals?

41. Traditional cultures believe that
    _____ inhabit trees, rocks,
    and rivers.

42. Which of these things do humans
    need to live and be healthy?
    (*Check all the right answers.*)

 A. Air

 B. More parking lots and fewer trees

 C. Water

 D. The sun's energy

 E. Shopping

 F. Soil

43. What are the "three *R*s" you can do to
    help the environment?

44. What are three other things you can
    do to help take care of the Earth?

Answers

1. Oxygen

2. False. We do the opposite—we breathe in oxygen and breathe out carbon dioxide.

3. Photosynthesis

4. Oxygen passes into the bloodstream through the walls of the air sacs.

5. Troposphere

6. Human activities

7. The ozone layer is a thin layer in the Earth's atmosphere that lies above the troposphere. It shields the Earth from much of the sun's harmful ultraviolet light rays.

8. It depends on the amount of greenhouse gases in the air. In the right amount, they keep the atmosphere warm enough for life. But if they build up above the amount that plants can absorb, they can cause global warming.

9. Inside your body cells

10. 1.5 to 2 L (quarts)—that's 6 to 8 glasses. Some of that water, though, comes from your food.

11. (D) Water is necessary for all your body processes, such as digestion, breathing, and blood circulation. As for the other answers, good taste is a plus but not a necessity for life. Water does not contain carbohydrates, and it won't cure warts. (If you're healthy, though, your body has a better chance of fighting off all kinds of diseases.)

12. All are possible because they're all part of the Earth's water cycle.

13. Fresh water

14. (A), (C), and (D) are all good ways. But don't try to save water by drinking less than you need. The idea is to stop wasting water.

15. True

16. Fats, carbohydrates, proteins, and certain vitamins and minerals. You also need water and fiber.

17. Weathering

18. Worms, beetles, ants, fungi, nematodes, springtails, and bacteria are only some of the many organisms you might find in the soil. Of course, you would need a microscope to see some of them.

19. Plants and animals contain nutrients. When they die, their bodies supply the soil with these nutrients, which new plants need to grow.

20. (C) is one way to keep soil healthy. The other answers are more likely to make the soil less healthy.

21. Grains, such as rice, wheat, and corn

22. The sun

23. The inner core. Unless you're sick, the temperature of your inner core will always stay very close to 37 °C (98 °F).

24. They learned how to control fire.

25. Because like fossils, they were formed from the remains of ancient plants and animals.

26. Metabolism, absorbing heat from the outside through your skin, and using energy from muscular movement, including shivering.

27. Some of the many ways you can use less energy are turning out lights when you're not using them, using energy-saving light bulbs, turning down the thermostat, recycling as much garbage as possible, and not buying things you don't need.

28. Habitat

29. Species

30. Salmon are food for animals such as bears, wolves, and eagles. After these animals have digested the salmon, they drop their feces in the forest. The droppings contain nutrients from the salmon. These nutrients go into the soil and help plants (such as trees) and animals grow.

31. (A) and (B) are necessary reasons; (C) may not be necessary, but it's a good reason, too.

32. Plants and animals interact with each other and with the air, soil, and water that are part of ecosystems. They depend on all these things to survive.

33. A time when many species are becoming extinct very rapidly

34. Human beings and their activities

35. They fuse (their contents mix).

36. Animals that live in groups

37. Love

38. False. Humans share many of their genes with all other animals and even plants.

39. Some of the reasons people tell creation stories are to tell them where they came from, to tell them why they were born, to teach them good ways to behave and live, to explain why there is cruelty and misfortune in the world, and to explain what happens when they die.

40. A bigger brain

41. Spirits

42. (A), (C), (D), and (F)

43. Reduce, Recycle, Reuse

44. See the list on page 136.

Italic page numbers point to information in pictures and text balloons.

ultraviolet light, 24, 27

The David Suzuki Foundation

The David Suzuki Foundation works through science and education to protect the diversity of nature and our quality of life, now and for the future.

With a goal of achieving sustainability within a generation, the Foundation collaborates with scientists, business and industry, academia, government and non-governmental organizations. We seek the best research to provide innovative solutions that will help build a clean, competitive economy that does not threaten the natural services that support all life.

The Foundation is a federally registered independent charity that is supported with the help of over 50,000 individual donors across Canada and around the world.

We invite you to become a member. For more information on how you can support our work, please contact us:

The David Suzuki Foundation
219–2211 West 4th Avenue
Vancouver, BC
Canada v6k 4s2
www.davidsuzuki.org
contact@davidsuzuki.org
Tel: 604-732-4228
Fax: 604-732-0752

Checks can be made payable to The David Suzuki Foundation. All donations are tax-deductible.

Canadian charitable registration: (BN) 12775 6716 RR0001
U.S. charitable registration: #94-3204049